Urban Battle Command in the 21st Century

Russell W. Glenn, Gina Kingston

Prepared for the United States Army

RAND ARROYO CENTER

The research described in this report was sponsored by the United States
Army under Contract No. DASW01-01-C-0003.

ISBN: 0-8330-3742-0

The RAND Corporation is a nonprofit research organization providing
objective analysis and effective solutions that address the challenges
facing the public and private sectors around the world. RAND's
publications do not necessarily reflect the opinions of its research clients
and sponsors.

RAND˙ is a registered trademark.

Published 2005 by the RAND Corporation
1776 Main Street, P.O. Box 2138, Santa Monica, CA 90407-2138
1200 South Hayes Street, Arlington, VA 22202-5050
201 North Craig Street, Suite 202, Pittsburgh, PA 15213-1516
RAND URL: http://www.rand.org/
To order RAND documents or to obtain additional information, contact
Distribution Services: Telephone: (310) 451-7002;
Fax: (310) 451-6915; Email: order@rand.org

Preface

Urban operations are among the most, if not the most, demanding of undertakings for a ground force. This is true whether combat, stability, or support considerations dominate the operation. The four functions of command; control; intelligence, surveillance, and reconnaissance; and communications are all fundamental to success in any environment, but the urban environment's dense populations, many manmade structures, and other challenges act to severely impede each in several ways. This study contemplates the nature of those challenges and proposes several recommendations to surmount them in both the short and longer terms.

The document will be of interest to individuals in the government, nongovernmental organizations, private volunteer organizations, and the commercial sector whose responsibilities include planning, policy, doctrine, training, and the conduct of actions undertaken in or near urban areas in both the immediate future and the longer term.

This research was sponsored by the U.S. Army Training and Doctrine Command Deputy Chief of Staff for Development and was conducted in RAND Arroyo Center's Force Development and Technology Program. RAND Arroyo Center, part of the RAND Corporation, is a federally funded research and development center sponsored by the United States Army.

For more information on RAND Arroyo Center, contact the Director of Operations (telephone 310-393-0411, extension 6419; FAX 310-451-6952; e-mail Marcy_Agmon@rand.org), or visit Arroyo's web site at http://www.rand.org/ard/.

Contents

Figures

Summary

Leaders of America's ground forces recognize the importance of putting themselves at the most critical point on a battlefield, for it is there that their experience, judgment, and demonstration of physical courage can best influence the outcome of deadly combat. Yet being forward has its costs. The tactical command posts (TOCs) that a commander establishes are hubs of information, intelligence, specialized insight, and communications. Leaving a TOC involves a level of trust: trust that subordinates and staff will inform the commander of important events by exception, that is, the commander is not informed of all events, but will be informed when something of sufficient importance takes place to warrant doing so. If the commander has left the TOC, it means that his ability to receive those messages is less consistent. A leader on the road or in the air has fewer means to send or receive information, and those messages have more chances to fall prey to the vagaries of geography or the myriad other demons that plague military communications. Even reaching the forward position does not resolve the dilemma. The commander is in one sense as well informed as is possible. The situation at his location is described by those most familiar with it. He sees the faces and senses the attitudes of his soldiers or marines. He surveys the ground with his own practiced eye. But the leader knows that he sees and understands but one part of his command. The cost of intimacy at one point is lesser understanding of all others.

Positioning oneself becomes a matter of judgment, risk, necessity, and gut feel. The same savvy that allows a leader to understand a situation while subordinates are overwhelmed provides a commander a sense of where he is most needed. The conundrum comes when the advantages of any given location still fall far short of a leader's needs, when he finds that none singly provides even the minimum acceptable level of awareness but moving to others does nothing to improve the situation. World War I commanders, so long (and sometimes justifiably) reviled for "hiding" in their distant headquarters, probably felt the pains of this quandary. They were torn between staying in the one place that provided them some understanding of the many miles of front for which they were responsible and a more forward location that gave them their only chance to directly influence events once a battle began. To move forward took them hours, left them virtually without communications, and permitted interaction with only a few handfuls of men at any one stop. Were something to occur elsewhere, the fate of their other soldiers was then in the hands of those less experienced, less in control of the implements of war.

The urban environment is not unlike World War I's Western Front in some regards. Though the distances between TOCs are far less and the dispersion of a command likely much reduced, buildings contrive to interfere with communications and limit line-of-sight so that visiting forward positions can enlighten a leader on only a small portion of the whole for which he is responsible. However, the complexity of the environment multiplies the challenges. The commander's World War I counterpart generally had little reason to worry about the welfare of multitudes of civilians or the condition of the battlefield when combat was over. He was fortunate in at least one way: he could focus almost exclusively on the conduct of battle with few distractions. How much different it is when one's actions influence the safety and survival of tens, hundreds, or even tens of thousands of noncombatants while the enemy is no less malevolent in his intentions.

In some ways the modern commander is fortunate. He is a member of a superior profession of arms, one now better informed by the lessons of history and better provided guidance by carefully considered doctrine. He himself is far better educated, as are those serving under him. Unfortunately, leaders remain less well prepared for urban contingencies despite the notable advances. Doctrine lags in its provision; in too many cases it actually works against proper conceptualization of the challenges inherent in urban operations. Even such basic concepts as "battle command" and "center of gravity" are inadequate to the task. Traditional thinking on task organizing units and providing them support to some extent breaks down. Tanks and infantry will still work side-by-side, but instead of three companies of one supporting another, it is more likely that a single armored vehicle works with a squad or platoon of foot soldiers. The resultant increase in the number of separate elements that commanders must oversee, support, and lead increases several fold, as do the complications in commanding them.

The original tasking that motivated this study asked that the authors consider the topic of "urban battle command." Unfortunately the current doctrine pertaining to battle command was found wanting. There are lessons to be taken from its deficiencies, however, and viewing the task from the perspective of command and leadership; control; intelligence, surveillance, and reconnaissance (ISR); and communications allowed the authors to address the sponsor's concerns with no loss in resolution. The task was further eased in that the team of which the authors are a part had already investigated urban reconnaissance and communications in previous work, permitting them to focus on the elements of command, leadership, and control more specifically. Each of these areas, and still to a lesser extent ISR and communications, find treatment in the body of this analysis. It was found that providing the results of the examination via seven primary recommendations helps in managing the many components such an undertaking demands. The seven are

- Look deeper in time and beyond military considerations during the backward planning process.
- Consider second- and higher-order effects during planning and war gaming.
- Doctrine asks lower-echelon leaders to look two levels up. Higher-echelon commanders need to consider the limits and

perspectives of same nation and other subordinate headquarters and units. Commanders at every echelon need to be conscious of the situation as it affects those at higher, lower, adjacent, joint, multinational, and interagency levels.

- Account for the language, cultural, procedural, and other differences that will impede the tempo and level of understanding when dealing with some coalition member units and other agencies.

- Be aware that urban densities compress the operational area and can result in more incidents of fratricide.

- Get the ROE right as quickly as possible.

- See the forest *and* selected trees.

The following simple examples illustrate some of the main concerns in each of these areas:

Look deeper in time and beyond military considerations during the backward planning process.

The density of responsibilities during urban operations means that backward planning from actions on the objective or a similar combat end state might be inadequate. The commander who today is victorious in urban combat tomorrow finds himself tasked with rebuilding the damage wrought. As such, it will stand that commander in good stead if he ensures that his force avoids damaging or destroying those elements of urban infrastructure that will help restore the city to postcombat normalcy. This requires identifying such assets before fighting starts (ideally). Therefore, determining what the city will have to look like after it is restored to normalcy is a better point from which to begin backward planning. Combat will require damage and destruction, but a leader will benefit if he can minimize the extent to which it interferes with his longer-term missions.

Consider second- and higher-order effects during planning and war gaming.

Urban areas have more physical, social, and other infrastructure per unit of space than do other environments. It then stands to reason that in an urban area, a change to one part of an infrastructure will be faster to affect its other parts. Commanders need to consider the residual impact of their actions several iterations removed from the primary effect sought. To provide a simplistic example, cutting off the water supply to a portion of a city occupied by the enemy with the intention of causing his surrender (the primary effect sought) could be effective. If the same area houses several thousand noncombatants, however, it is likely that the enemy will seize what little potable water there is for his own use. The civilians will be forced to seek other sources of fluids for consumption (a second-order effect) that may be unclean. This may in turn result in an outbreak of cholera (third-order effect) that, once the enemy surrenders, results in the friendly-force military commander having to provide medical care for the noncombatants (fourth-order effect).

Doctrine asks lower-echelon leaders to look two levels up. Higher-echelon commanders need to consider the limits and perspectives of same nation and other subordinate headquarters and units.

The complexity of the urban environment translates to greater demands on intelligence collection, processing, and dissemination as well as complicating other staff processes. The tempo of operations can be very high when measured in terms of the number of activities per unit time. The lower the echelon, the less likely it is to be manned with the numbers and expertise to handle these greater demands. Leaders at higher echelons may have to assume responsibility for some of the tasks normally handled at lower levels, or they should consider otherwise reducing the burden on those at subordinate echelons by better screening the intelligence or other products sent to them.

Account for the language, cultural, procedural, and other differences that will impede the tempo and level of understanding when dealing with some coalition member units and other agencies.

Australians operating in Dili, East Timor found that working with coalition members offers both benefits and challenges, much as did the Americans in Mogadishu in 1993. Traditional staff procedures might well require modification in the interest of greater efficiency and effectiveness. Units from various militaries that might work together should not find that their first experience of doing so is when they are under fire. The types of barriers to smooth operations that the United States experienced over many years when transitioning to greater jointness still influence multinational and interagency undertakings.

Be aware that urban densities compress the operational area and can result in more incidents of fratricide.

During tactical movements, factors such as noise, interruptions of lines of sight, extremely short decision times, and the multiplicity of alleys, corridors, and streets make control very difficult. Similar challenges exist during virtually any operation in a built-up area and influence the operational as well as the tactical level of war. Training and rules of engagement (ROE) will help to reduce the incidence of accidentally engaging friendly forces and noncombatants, but modifications of control methods and development of junior leaders before deployment to such contingencies will also be essential.

Get the ROE right as quickly as possible.

The same ROE that help to save fellow soldiers' and civilians' lives can act to endanger those of the men and women restrained by them. History offers repeated examples of ROE designed to reduce the damage caused to buildings and human life that have the unfortunate consequence of costing soldiers' lives because they too greatly interfere with actions essential to survival in combat. The longer the period of adjustment, the greater is the risk for those in contact with the enemy. There is a need to carefully design and thereafter monitor ROE such that an appropriate balance is found quickly.

See the forest *and* selected trees.

The complexity of urban operations as demonstrated, to some extent, by the above examples can overwhelm the individual rifleman, his commander, and all others between and in support. There is a need to focus both on individual points of particular mission importance and the bigger picture. The individual points can be physical (a sniper, particular building, or element of infrastructure), social (a particularly influential individual or important link between groups), political, economic, or otherwise. Because it seems that the individual parts are inevitably intermeshed (as already highlighted above), focusing on the points to the exclusion of how they fit into one or more greater wholes can be counterproductive to mission accomplishment. Avoiding being overwhelmed and retaining a macro perspective do not come naturally. Most individuals are more comfortable "in the weeds" than they are assuming a perspective requiring a more comprehensive scope of understanding. Recognizing how to maintain a balance between the detailed and general and doing so in practice require training and application. It is an area that receives too little attention.

Urban operations make extraordinary demands on those undertaking military actions in today's towns and cities. Those demands encompass virtually every aspect of a mission, reaching across arms, services, and agencies. The responsibility for establishing the conditions for success and then overseeing them through to accomplishment lies with commanders and their staffs. This report considers how this might best be done.

Acknowledgments

The authors are grateful to those who provided us with information or granted us interviews: LtCol (USMC, retired) John Allison, COL (USA, retired) Johnny Brooks, Col Jay Bruder, COL Lee Gore, Dr. Todd Helmus, Chief Dan Lindsay, Battalion Chief John P. Miller, LTC Doug Ridenour, LTC Jared L. Ware, MAJ John Simeoni, LTC J.D. Wilson, and BG (IDF, retired) Nachum Zaken.

Two men combined military expertise and academic insight to provide outstanding formal reviews of this study. The efforts of Gideon Avidor (Brigadier General, Israeli Defense Force, retired) and David Oaks (Lieutenant Colonel, U.S. Army Reserve) make this a better offering to our readers. The same is true of the informal review kindly provided by Lieutenant Colonel Mike Chura.

The authors also thank Terri Perkins and Nikki Shacklett, whose efforts in rapidly turning the rough into the polished are unsurpassed.

Glossary

2d, 82d	2nd Division and 82nd Division respectively
AARC	Allied Command Europe Rapid Reaction Corps
APC	Armored Personnel Carrier
ARVN	Army of the Republic of Vietnam
AWE	Advanced Warfighting Experiment
BG	Brigadier General
BOS	Battlefield Operating Systems
C2	Command and Control
CA	Civil Affairs
CINC	Commander in Chief
CMOC	Civil-Military Operations Center
COL	Colonel
FM	Field Manual
FSO	Fire Support Officer
GPS	Global Positioning System
HF	High Frequency
HIDACZ	High-Density Airspace Control Zone
HMMWV	High-Mobility Multipurpose Wheeled Vehicle

HUMINT	Human Intelligence
ICRC	International Committee of the Red Cross
IFV	Infantry Fighting Vehicle
INTERFET	International Force East Timor
IPB	Intelligence Preparation of the Battlefield
ISR	Intelligence, Surveillance, and Reconnaissance
JCF	Joint Contingency Force
JTF	Joint Task Force
LAV	Light Armored Vehicle
LNO	Liaison Officer
LTC	Lieutenant Colonel
LTG	Lieutenant General
MAJ	Major
MASINT	Measurements and Signatures Intelligence
MEDEVAC	Medical Evacuation
MG	Major General
MOUT	Military Operations on Urbanized Terrain
MPAT	Multipurpose Anti-tank
NATO	North Atlantic Treaty Organization
NCO	Non-Commissioned Officer
NGO	Nongovernmental Organization
NIMA	National Imagery Mapping Agency
NOFORN	Not Releasable to Foreign Nationals
NVG	Night-Vision Goggles
OIF	Operation Iraqi Freedom
OPCON	Operational Control

PSYOP	Psychological Operations
PVO	Private Voluntary Organization
QRF	Quick Reaction Force
ROE	Rules of Engagement
ROZ	Restricted Operations Zone
RSTA	Reconnaissance, Surveillance, and Target Acquisition
SIGINT	Signals Intelligence
SOAR (A)	Special Operations Aviation Regiment (Airborne)
SOP	Standard Operating Procedure
TACON	Tactical Control
TF	Task Force
TOC	Tactical Operations Center
TOW	Tube-Launched, Optically-Tracked, Wire-Guided
TRADOC	Training and Doctrine Command
TTP	Tactics, Techniques, and Procedures
UAV	Unmanned Aerial Vehicle
UGV	Unmanned Ground Vehicle
UN	United Nations
UNITAF	United Nations Task Force
UNOSOM II	United Nations Operations Somalia II
USFORSOM	U.S. Forces Somalia
VHF	Very High Frequency

CHAPTER ONE

Setting the Stage: The Urban Battle Command Environment

Americans have worked at war since the seventeenth century, to protect themselves from the Indians, to win their independence from George III, to make themselves one country, to win the whole of their continent, to extinguish autocracy and dictatorship in the world outside. It is not their favoured form of work. Left to themselves, Americans build, cultivate, bridge, dam, canalise, invent, teach, manufacture, think, write, lock themselves in struggle with the eternal challenges that man has chosen to confront, and with an intensity not known elsewhere on the globe. Bidden to make war their work, Americans shoulder the burden with intimidating purpose. There is, I have said, an American mystery, the nature of which I only begin to perceive. If I were obliged to define it, I would say it is the ethos of work as an end in itself. War is a form of work, and America makes war, however reluctantly, however unwillingly, in a particularly workmanlike way.

John Keegan
Fields of Battle, 1995

The job at hand in the dust-choked streets and smoke-filled air would demand the most of this American ethos. Courage, commitment, perseverance, delegation, patience, and leadership: all would be called on. And all would be answered. It was October 1993 in Mogadishu, Somalia, during United Nations Operations Somalia II (UNOSOM II). Soldiers from the 10th Mountain Division, 160th Special Operations Aviation Regiment (Airborne), and other units were fighting to support and retrieve U.S. Army Rangers and Delta Force personnel who had in turn sought to rescue comrades in downed aircraft. The Americans had no tanks or infantry fighting vehicles in the city. Previous efforts to reach the brutal fighting via High-Mobility Multipurpose Wheeled Vehicles (HMMWVs) and trucks had resulted in confusion and casualties.

Mogadishu, October 3–4, 1993: A Tactical Leadership Vignette

Lieutenant Mark Hollis, a platoon leader in the 10th Mountain Division relief force, had just received guidance on how the next phase of the operation would take place. Hollis thought the plan

> was simple: Pakistani tanks would lead Malaysian [armored personnel carriers] carrying 2d Battalion soldiers. Company A would attack to break through to [Task Force] Ranger. The column began movement around 2145 hours, with the Pakistani T55 tanks in the lead.[1]

But this was urban combat. Hollis, riding in one of those armored personnel carriers, found that navigating to the crash site

> was impossible; every time I tried to look out, I was thrown in a different direction.
>
> The vehicle began to pick up speed. We started going over curbs and obstacles in the road, which again threw us around. Unknown to me, at the same time the first vehicle, which held the 1st Squad leader, and my vehicle, the second, began pulling away from the rest of the column. The commander's placement of his HMMWV, the third vehicle in the march order, was the only thing that kept the rest of the Malaysians from following the runaway lead vehicles. This effectively separated me and my two lead squads from the rest of the company. We did not see the rest of the company again until the next morning.

---

[1] Mark A. B. Hollis, "Platoon Under Fire: Mogadishu, October 1993," *Infantry*, January–April 1998, pp. 29–31. "2145 hours" corresponds to 9:45 P.M.

At this time, I was totally disoriented and had not realized we were on our own. Being bounced around in an armored vehicle made it difficult to tell which way I was going, while the explosions outside made communication with the company commander virtually impossible . . . .

Three men were injured; one of them took a round in the chest and died later in Germany when surgeons tried to remove the bullet . . . .

The location from which I chose to command and control our vehicles' movement was unsatisfactory. I learned that I should avoid any location where my field of view is limited. If I had taken the assistant driver's position instead, I would have known immediately when my element broke contact with the rest of the company . . . .

A platoon leader sent into a theater of operation needs to know and understand the equipment he may be using. I had never seen or heard of a German Condor [armored personnel carrier] until the day of execution. Finding out how to open the door to a vehicle 15 minutes before rolling out the gate is not the way to start a mission. A platoon leader needs to coordinate through his company commander to arrange a time when the allied forces can come over and teach his soldiers about their equipment. This is particularly significant at a time when operations with other United Nations forces are becoming more frequent . . . . How do we communicate with those who do not speak English in the midst of battle, with no interpreters available?

Mogadishu, October 3–4, 1993: An Operational Level Command Vignette

Communications failures, the inability to see, unfamiliarity with coalition member equipment and language, and an aggressive enemy thwarted Lieutenant Hollis's ability to control his force. The challenges confronting those senior in his chain of command differed in character but not consequence.

The first priority for LTC John Allison, a Joint Staff planner during operations in Somalia, was to try to understand "who the

players were in the hierarchy, who reports to who from national strategic to tactical. Each country had their own reporting chain and interests."[2] Some countries had a dual reporting structure, some were
reporting through an alliance, and some forces were operating directly
under national control. Some of the U.S. forces in Mogadishu were
notionally commanded by the Turkish United Nations (UN) com-
mandeer General Bir.[3] The Deputy UN Commander was U.S. Army
Lieutenant General Thomas Montgomery. Not unusual for the military forces of any nation assigned to a UN force, Montgomery also
served as the Commander, U.S. Forces Somalia, a position in which
he reported not to Bir but rather the Commander in Chief of U.S.
Central Command in Tampa, Florida, General Hoar. His title notwithstanding, Montgomery did not command all U.S. forces in
Mogadishu, much less all of Somalia. The Quick Reaction Force
(QRF) from the 10th Mountain Division, the organization he would
have to rely on in a short-notice, high-threat situation, was under
Montgomery's *tactical control* but not his *operational control*.[4] In
short, General Montgomery could influence how this important element of his force was used in specific situations but could not dictate

---

[2] John Allison, interview with Gina Kingston, Arlington, Virginia, June 6, 2003.

[3] The following summary of command relationships in Somalia relies on "Ambush in
Mogadishu: Interview—General Thomas Montgomery (Ret.)," *Frontline*, Public Broadcasting System, undated, http://www.pbs.org/wgbh/pages/frontline/shows/ambush/interviews/
montgomery.html, accessed May 30, 2003.

[4] Tactical control (TACON) is "command authority over assigned or attached forces or
commands, or military capability or forces made available for tasking, that is limited to the
detailed and, usually, local direction and control of movement or maneuvers necessary to
accomplish missions or tasks assigned. Tactical control is inherent in operational control."
Operational control (OPCON) is "the authority to perform those functions of command
over subordinate forces involving organization and employing commands and forces, assigning tasks, designating objectives, and giving authoritative direction necessary to accomplish the mission. Operational control includes authoritative direction over all aspects of
military operations and joint training necessary to accomplish missions assigned to the command . . . . Operational control normally provides full authority to organize commands and
forces and to employ those forces as the commander in operational control considers necessary to accomplish assigned missions." Joint Pub 1-02, *Department of Defense Dictionary of
Military and Associated Terms,* April 12, 2001 (as amended through May 23, 2003), pp. 385
and 519.

Figure 1.1
Command Arrangements in Somalia

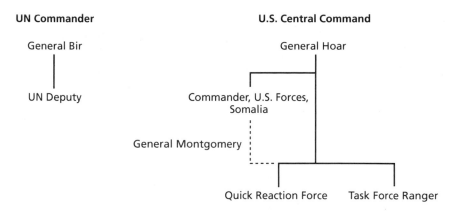

NOTE: The dashed line indicates tactial control.

how best to organize its forces or combine them with those from other organizations in the interest of mission accomplishment. That authority remained with General Hoar. Montgomery had neither tactical nor operational control over yet another significant U.S. military capability in Mogadishu: Task Force Ranger, consisting of Ranger Regiment, Delta, Task Force 160, and other special operations elements. MG William F. Garrison commanded TF Ranger and reported directly to General Hoar in Tampa.

That there was an imperfect response to the difficult situation of October 3–4, 1993 at higher as well as Lieutenant Hollis's echelon should therefore come as no surprise. Generals Hoar, Montgomery, and Garrison were further hampered by the political decision not to bring U.S. armor or mechanized forces into theater; the QRF had to rely on Pakistani and Malaysian coalition forces to extract the outnumbered Americans when the enemy's resistance proved too tough for trucks and HMMWVs. Those multinational forces did not answer directly to General Hoar, General Montgomery, or General Garrison. Instead, they were under the command of their own nations' military leaders in Karachi and Kuala Lumpur. George S. Patton once likened combat to an orchestra in which every instrument complements others to create an effective symphony of violence. The cacophony of armed forces in October 1993 Mogadishu answered to at least four conductors.

Command structure was only one part of the issue. Another part was the resultant control difficulties. Another was insufficient combined arms and multinational training. Another was the unavailability of U.S. armored and mechanized forces. Yet another was communications. And a very significant part was the success of enemy tactics. But a proper command structure that facilitates control and promotes well-conceived training is better able to identify shortfalls and develop solutions that much abet the defeat of even the most able of enemies.

The U.S. Army Training and Doctrine Command (TRADOC) Pamphlet 525-4-0, *The United States Army Objective Force Maneuver Sustainment Support Concept,* describes how the challenges of urban operations compare with those in other environments. The list is incomplete, but it provides further substantiation that missions such as the one conducted in Mogadishu are among the most difficult of military undertakings. The TRADOC authors conclude that urban contingencies require

> more [Public Affairs Officer] support . . . more Civil Affairs (CA) activity . . . more frequent reconstitution of forces . . . . Expect ammunition consumption to rise by a factor of at least three. Weapons maintenance will increase; maintenance goes to supported units, not evacuated; periods for soldier rest and recuperation are more frequent; expect high casualty rates; expect operations to be more time-consuming; expect infrastructure to be extremely vulnerable; and expect support for forcible entry operations. Medical and health services are critically stressed. Expect more injuries, disease, and psychological casualties. Expect terrorist acts.[5]

---

[5] TRADOC Pamphlet 525-4-0, *The United States Army Objective Force Maneuver Sustainment Support Concept,* Fort Monroe, VA: U.S. Army Training and Doctrine Command, Version 12-03-01a, p. 18.

Commanders conducting urban operations must expect all of these and more in the way of challenges. These leaders need to prepare their units for such demands before they deploy. The remainder of this report provides material that the authors trust will be of value in that regard.

CHAPTER TWO

A Call for Moving Urban Command and Control Doctrine into the 21st Century

> The teams and staffs through which the modern commander absorbs information and exercises his authority must be a beautifully interlocked, smooth-working mechanism. Ideally, the whole should be practically a single mind.
>
> General Dwight D. Eisenhower

Introduction

Operations in Mogadishu provide a pertinent backdrop for a consideration of urban battle command. There was far more to these operations than just those two days in October 1993. Personnel from all four U.S. armed services and those of many other nations worked for many months to bring relief to starving Somalis, introduce stability, and deliver a cruel clan head to justice. Together the sequence of the several operations and actions shown in Figure 2.1 might have achieved the status of a campaign had there been sufficient coherency of political guidance and operational continuity to link them logically.[1]

---

[1] A campaign is "a series of related military operations aimed at accomplishing a strategic or operational objective within a given time and space." Joint Pub 1-02, *Department of Defense Dictionary of Military and Associated Terms*, April 12, 2001 (as amended through May 23, 2003), p. 76.

Figure 2.1
U.S. Operations in Somalia

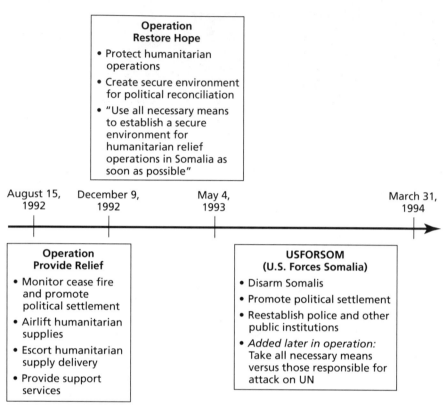

Operation Restore Hope
- Protect humanitarian operations
- Create secure environment for political reconciliation
- "Use all necessary means to establish a secure environment for humanitarian relief operations in Somalia as soon as possible"

August 15, 1992   December 9, 1992   May 4, 1993   March 31, 1994

Operation Provide Relief
- Monitor cease fire and promote political settlement
- Airlift humanitarian supplies
- Escort humanitarian supply delivery
- Provide support services

USFORSOM (U.S. Forces Somalia)
- Disarm Somalis
- Promote political settlement
- Reestablish police and other public institutions
- *Added later in operation:* Take all necessary means versus those responsible for attack on UN

RAND *MG181A-2.1*

SOURCES: Kenneth Allard, *Somalia Operations: Lessons Learned,* Fort McNair, Washington, D.C.: National Defense University Press, 1995; "Operation Provide Relief," Military Analysis Network, http://www.fas.org/man/dod-101/ops/provide_relief.htm, accessed July 2, 2003; and "Operation Restore Hope," Military Analysis Network, http://www.fas.org/man/dod-101/opsrestore_hope.htm, accessed July 2, 2003.
NOTE: USFORSOM is U.S. Forces Somalia.

These months of U.S. and UN force commitment in Mogadishu made demands similar to what future commanders are sure to experience in urban areas worldwide. Americans had conducted and supported missions involving the gamut of support, stability, defensive, and offensive operations during their time in the Horn of Africa.

While there were shortfalls with regard to the command of these enterprises, there was also much in the way of success. Cooperation between military forces and private volunteer organizations may not have been perfect. However, the United Nations Task Force's (UNITAF) establishment of a Civil-Military Operations Center (CMOC) helped to ensure that both civilian and military efforts to aid Mogadishu's suffering were moving in the same general direction despite their not always sharing identical approaches or motivations. U.S. and multinational commanders developed liaison ties that were a significant element in reducing operational conflicts and misunderstandings.[2] Progress beyond these basic levels of cooperation proved too difficult to attain in many circumstances. Various nations refused to allow their forces to support actions in the city of Mogadishu, restricting personnel to areas away from the capital.[3] The situation was much like that in Bosnia, about which a commander commented that "every troop contributing nation had its own national command structure within the main UN staff, and each nation had its own political agenda as well as a chief of contingent who held the national red card."[4] In this and many other regards, Mogadishu offers lessons that commanders are well advised to consider now rather than after they are committed to an urban area in a domestic or overseas theater. The following pages contemplate such challenges in the context of battle command. The discussion begins with a look at battle command and several related constructs designed to support a commander in analyzing, planning, and conducting operations. In several cases, joint and service doctrine have defined these concepts so narrowly as to keep them from meeting their full potential when applied to undertakings in modern cities. Recommendations for remedying

---

[2] Norman L. Cooling, *Shaping the Battlespace to Win the Street Fight*, thesis for the School of Advanced Military Studies, Fort Leavenworth, KS, 2000, p. 74.

[3] *Logistics in a Peace Enforcement Environment: Operation Continue Hope Lessons Learned*, Fort Leavenworth, KS: U.S. Army Center for Army Lessons Learned, November 16, 1993, p. 12.

[4] David Potts, ed., *The Big Issue: Command and Combat in the Information Age*, The Strategic and Combat Studies Institute Occasional Paper Number 45, March 2002, p. 36.

these self-inflicted shortcomings follow their identification. Thereafter the study looks in turn at four functional areas inherent in battle command: (1) leadership and command, (2) control, (3) intelligence, surveillance, and reconnaissance (ISR), and (4) communications. The discussion takes into account how urban environments present challenges to each functional area and how a force might overcome those challenges. A general discussion of findings and recommendations concludes the document.

The primary focus of the pages to follow is on areas (1) and (2). ISR and communications are essential to successful battle command, but they are the supporting cast that facilitates command and control. The authors also do not wish to repeat material presented in previous RAND Corporation urban studies. ISR is touched on, albeit in a limited manner, in the 2003 *Honing the Keys to the City: Refining the United States Marine Corps Reconnaissance Force for Urban Ground Operations*.[5] Similarly, communications difficulties and possible solutions are addressed in *Freeing Mercury's Wings: Improving Tactical Communications in Cities*.[6] Readers desiring to delve into either topic more thoroughly are invited to refer to these efforts.

The focus of consideration is primarily near term: What needs to be done *now* to improve U.S. Army battle command capabilities? It is also urban-oriented, but many of the observations and recommendations apply equally to other environments no less than the world's villages, towns, and cities. With this last caveat, we turn to relevant current and emerging doctrine.

---

[5] Russell W. Glenn et al., *Honing the Keys to the City: Refining the United States Marine Corps Reconnaissance Force for Urban Ground Operations,* Santa Monica, CA: RAND Corporation, MR-1628-USMC, 2003.

[6] Sean J. A. Edwards, *Freeing Mercury's Wings: Improving Tactical Communications in Cities*, Santa Monica, CA: RAND Corporation, MR-1316-A, 2001.

Flaws in the Foundation: Shortcomings in Doctrine

It is necessary to define the term "battle command" and discuss several related elements before asking how urban areas affect the exercise of urban battle command and what can be done to favorably influence that process.

Field Manual (FM) 3.0, *Operations,* defines battle command as "the exercise of command in operations against a hostile, thinking enemy."[7] This, the definition that should underlie this study, has two principal elements. First, it is commander-focused. Such an emphasis is encouraging given the aforementioned problems of command during operations in Mogadishu. Second, battle command requires the existence of "a hostile, thinking enemy," something that should not surprise the reader given that there is a need to distinguish "battle command" from a generic concept of "command." Otherwise the term "command" alone would suffice.

This second element, the requirement that an individual exercising battle command have a foil, a "thinking enemy," at first glance seems innocuous enough. Yet the examples of Hurricane Andrew relief in Florida, support to California authorities during the 1992 Los Angeles riots, recent stability operations in Haiti, and virtually any other urban operation in which American forces have recently been involved demonstrate that

1. Many urban operations do not involve a human adversary.
2. There are many challenges present during urban operations that are independent of or only marginally related to the enemy even when a foe does exist.

Case 1 is not especially problematic. One can claim that such contingencies do not make the demands on an individual that require him (or her) to consider the additional complexity introduced by

---

[7] Field Manual 3-0, *Operations,* Washington, D.C.: Headquarters, Department of the Army, June 2001, p. 5-1; and Field Manual 6-0, *Mission Command: Command and Control of Army Forces,* Approved Final Draft, Washington, D.C.: Headquarters, Department of the Army, October 2002, p. 4-80.

having to deal with an enemy. "Normal" command will suffice. Case 2 is more provocative. There are occasions when a company or battalion commander will be able to focus exclusively on his enemy during urban operations. But even at these lowest of command echelons, an organization always has to be prepared to deal with the other demands of urban operations: providing care and security for noncombatants, maintaining some semblance of stability and order, or considering the implications of ongoing operations on postcombat recovery.

It is worth taking a moment to consider separately the definition of "command" (which is itself a component of "battle command"). It is defined as "the authority a commander in military service lawfully exercises over subordinates by virtue of rank and assignment."[8] Substituting this definition for "command" directly into that for battle command, the latter becomes "the exercise of the authority a commander in military service lawfully exercises over subordinates by virtue of rank and assignment in operations against a hostile, thinking enemy." Stating the definition in this manner better highlights a key element of battle command: the enemy is merely an environmental factor. The object of battle command is the commander's subordinates. The question is therefore not one of how a commander thinks or how he visualizes the area of operations when "against a hostile, thinking enemy," but rather how he exercises authority over subordinates because such an enemy influences an organization's activities.

It is not the intention of this study to question the validity of battle command as a concept. However, the coincidence of the above-highlighted simultaneous demands on commanders during many urban contingencies makes it worthwhile to consider whether the concept introduces an unnecessary delineation between the leadership and management of subordinates performing a combat task vice those involved in actions in which the enemy is not a primary factor. In case 1 (no human adversary), our commander provides care and security for noncombatants, maintains some semblance of stabil-

---

[8] Ibid., p. 5-1.

ity and order, considers the implications of ongoing operations on postcombat recovery, and handles whatever other responsibilities he might have. In case 2 he is responsible for all tasks encompassed in case 1 and now also has to deal with a thinking enemy. Given the current doctrinal definition of battle command, there is an implication that the commander somehow switches on and off between "command" and "battle command" depending on whether a thinking enemy influences the decision under consideration. Such an argument does not seem to survive careful scrutiny.

An astute reader will ask why the authors concern themselves with this issue, and in particular, why this argument would apply to urban contingencies and not others. The response is one related to proximity or, stated differently, to density. Cities tend to compress the multiple tasks inherent in providing support, maintaining stability, and waging combat into lesser space. A soldier is more likely to come across a noncombatant in need of aid while he is at the same time hunting his foe. A civilian vehicle approaching from down a street might or might not pose a threat. Although the same types of events occur in more open and less densely populated areas, they are less frequent. Operations Mogadishu in 1993 and Baghdad in 2003 demonstrate that support, stability, and combat activities are likely to occur simultaneously and close together during urban operations. A commander will rarely be able to focus exclusively on only one. Open areas do not generally present this same density of simultaneous demands. There an individual is more often able to concentrate on combat alone, leaving the rare support or stability concern to the executive officer, first sergeant, civil affairs officer, or command sergeant major. Thus while the above argument has application to actions in any environment, its consideration has greater immediate importance when the surroundings are urban.

"Battle command," the concept underlying this study, therefore seems not fully to fit the demands of urban operations. It is not that the combat talents of a commander are in any less demand. Rather, they are only some of a much greater combination of talents that he will have to demonstrate if he is to succeed during urban contingencies. He will have to be adept at destroying his enemy, negotiating with local government representatives, and coordinating his operations with those of indigenous community services. Urban warfare introduces a variety of challenges not frequently faced in other environments, and it does so in greater measure. Whereas commanders of the past seldom needed to concern themselves with civilians and post-hostility recovery while engaging their opponents, 21st century urban operations will increasingly demand this and more of America's warriors. The "management of violence" might still distinguish a soldier's profession from others, but success at such management alone is rarely sufficient to fully meet the demands of modern missions and objectives.[9] Commanders now must also preserve noncombatant life, not unduly damage civilian infrastructure, and be ready to maintain civilian order even before the enemy is completely defeated. In other environments the military commander may be able to define success as seizing the military objective. That will generally be only the initial phase of an urban operation; the greatest challenges will still lie ahead. "Battle command" seems overly simplistic; the commander in a city confronts a far more complex collection of demands than that addressed by the concept of battle command.

Battle command is not the only doctrinal concept to suffer when viewed through the lens of urban operations. Processes, terms, and concepts designed to aid commanders in decisionmaking need to account for the mix of missions and tasks a commander is likely to find confronting him in a city. His challenges will differ in type and character; his tools for addressing those challenges should be sufficiently flexible to account for that variation.

Unfortunately the commander's "tool box" has too many implements designed for decades now past, eras in which urban operations were the exception rather than the norm they are rapidly becoming. There is great value in the intellectual exchanges that debate what Clausewitz meant by "center of gravity" and how it applies today. The arguments should not preclude adapting the theorist's con-

---

[9] The term "management of violence" to delineate the military profession is from Samuel P. Huntington, *The Soldier and the State: The Theory and Politics of Civil-Military Relations*, New York: Vintage, 1957, p. 11.

cept to maintain its relevance. That it was one thing in 1831 need not preclude its being another in the twenty-first century. Good military theory is adaptive rather than rigid in adherence to its source. Its users appreciate the origins of concepts without being bound by them. Current U.S. military doctrine defines center of gravity as "those characteristics, capabilities, or localities from which a military force, organization, or individual derives its freedom of action, physical strength, or will to fight."[10] This definition is respectful of Clausewitz's intentions with a center of gravity as "the hub of all power and movement on which everything depends"[11] while at once moving well beyond its conception as the point at which "the mass is concentrated most densely."[12] The difficulty is that the U.S. doctrinal definition seems to have failed to move progress sufficiently from center of gravity as a Napoleonic, force-on-force concept. It restricts a commander to considering only entities that influence *military* forces, organizations, or individuals if taken literally.

But what of today's urban operations (or any operation for that matter) that involve no opposing military force? Is the concept of center of gravity denied a commander in such instances despite its being a valuable tool in determining where the most critical, mission-vital element of a situation lies? It seems that a mission requiring the feeding of a city's starving thousands could benefit from a center of gravity analysis. A center of gravity definition modified by as small a change as removing "military" would open its use to this and many other situations commonplace during military operations in the past two decades (and very likely to be characteristic of many yet to come). Being able to correctly determine whether maintaining open transportation routes, ensuring means of communicating with the public, coordinating for police support, or some other element of a food supply mission is most vital will be crucial to success. Thinking

---

[10] Joint Pub 1-02, *Department of Defense Dictionary of Military and Associated Terms*, Washington, D.C.: Joint Chiefs of Staff, April 12, 2003 (as amended through May 23, 2003), p. 80.

[11] Carl von Clausewitz, *On War*, Princeton: Princeton University Press, 1976, pp. 595–596.

[12] Ibid., p. 485.

in terms of a "support center of gravity" will unquestionably facilitate mission accomplishment. The definition of center of gravity should encompass such broader needs. In truth, elements of emerging U.S. Army doctrine are already moving toward a less restrictive definition, as evidenced by this excerpt from FM 3-20.96, *RSTA Squadron*:

> The troop must clearly understand the threat—be it conventional forces, paramilitary, terrorist, or organized crime . . . . The squadron should be very concerned with understanding the needs of the local populace . . . . The center of gravity during operations may be the civilian inhabitants themselves.[13]

From the perspective of psychological operations, civil affairs, or the long-term establishment of stability, beliefs, ideologies, predispositions, ignorance, or other less-than-physical elements could be the ultimate barrier to mission accomplishment.[14]

The center of gravity is the key to mission success. Destroying, controlling, unbalancing, or otherwise overcoming it is necessary to accomplishing a force's objectives. But a center of gravity may not be directly accessible to attack or influence. Alternatively, it might be too strong to destroy or unbalance. In such cases a commander must find another way of accomplishing his mission. He must influence the center of gravity but do it indirectly. There is a construct that helps to identify the means of so doing: decisive points. Imagine that the center of gravity, that which the commander must unbalance, is a wall.

---

[13] Field Manual 3-20.96, *RSTA Squadron,* 2nd Coordinating Draft, Fort Knox, KY: U.S. Army Armor Center, undated, pp. 3–22. "RSTA" is Reconnaissance, Surveillance, and Target Acquisition.

[14] The RAND Arroyo Urban Operations Team has considered the issues of urban centers of gravity and decisive points repeatedly over the past several years. In addition to the relevant arguments only briefly summarized here, its members forward the proposition that the two concepts are inadequate to the task of identifying those physical, social, economic, or other highly significant elements pertinent to meeting friendly force or coalition objectives. They propose the addition of "critical points" to the mix of constructs helpful in understanding and addressing the challenges inherent in urban undertakings. Critical points, defined as "points or other elements that could have an extraordinary influence on the achievement of objectives," include centers of gravity and decisive points as subsets. For further discussion, see Russell W. Glenn, *Managing Complexity During Urban Operations: Visualizing the Elephant,* Santa Monica, CA: RAND Corporation, DB-430-A, 2004.

But this wall is too strong to topple regardless of how hard one pushes against it. It cannot be defeated or unbalanced directly. The insightful commander therefore seeks indirect ways of neutralizing the problem. He determines which footers beneath the wall or which abutments that hold it erect are the most important. By removing these he causes the wall to fall. The footers and abutments are decisive points: those points of support or leverage that, when attacked or otherwise influenced, precipitate the collapse of the center of gravity. While this example illustrates the use of decisive points to topple a physical center of gravity, the concept applies as well to nonphysical centers of gravity.[15]

The urban applications of the decisive point concept are myriad. One could justifiably argue that Saddam Hussein was the coalition foe's center of gravity during Operation Iraqi Freedom. Yet much as was the case with Manuel Noriega in 1989 Panama, there was no guarantee that Hussein could be immediately toppled. Therefore an alternative means of neutralizing the center of gravity had to be found. What were the decisive points that supported Hussein and kept him in power? Other key members of his Baath party and selected Republican Guards elements both qualified, and both were

---

[15] One of this document's reviewers, Brigadier General (IDF, rct.) Gideon Avidor, argues that "the problem with Clausewitz's definition is that there is ONE source from [which all power derives]. In urban battle it does not exist." Furthermore, there are situations, e.g., those "dealing with terror or ethical issues" in which there is not a single COG; "there are several sources of power and influence that might create virtual COG." He goes on to state that such centers can be mobile, virtual in character, and can change form, making it almost impossible to destroy through direct attack. Further, he notes that virtual centers can revive fairly easily and quickly. General Avidor suggests that alternative ways of conceptualizing combat are necessary.

Both General Avidor and members of the RAND Arroyo Urban Operations Team have been considering challenges regarding critical points or nodes in urban operations for some time. General Avidor spoke on the topic during an urban conference at RAND Corporation headquarters in Santa Monica, California, in 2001. See Gideon Avidor, "The Revolution in Military Affairs: From Landscape and Linear Dimension to Systems and Centers of Gravity," in Russell W. Glenn (ed.), *Ready for Armageddon: Proceedings of the 2001 RAND Arroyo-U.S. Army ACTD-CETO-USMC Non-Lethal and Urban Operations Program Urban Operations Conference,* Santa Monica, CA: RAND Corporation, 2002, pp. 25–32. For RAND work on the subject, refer to Glenn, *Managing Complexity During Urban Operations: Visualizing the Elephant.*

attacked. But military operations did not end with cessation of major hostilities and the effective elimination of Hussein as the Iraqi leader, just as responsibilities in Panama did not cease with the removal of Manuel Noriega. There was little to establish and maintain security in the absence of the pre-war Iraqi security and police establishments. Baghdad was the most prominent case in point. Many of the city's residents soon began demonstrating for U.S. forces to depart.[16] For demonstrative purposes, assume that "mistrust of American intentions" was the center of gravity in seeking to reestablish urban (and, by extension, nationwide) security. Directly attacking the mistrust might have been impossible. It might have been counterproductive (e.g., providing aid in hopes of winning hearts and minds could have misfired if cultural, social, or religious norms were violated). Identifying and influencing decisive points could be the preferred way to influence the citizenry in the interest of short- and long-term stability in such situations. Seeking influential religious and social leaders, perhaps even working through pre-established private volunteer organizations, might have better served coalition interests. There is evidence that this approach is being adopted in some areas as stability operations continue in early 2004 in Iraqi urban areas.

Unfortunately, the doctrinal definition of "decisive point" is even less helpful than that for center of gravity in such applications. U.S. joint doctrine defines a decisive point as "a geographic place, specific key event, critical system, or function that allows commanders to gain a marked advantage over an enemy and greatly influence the outcome of an attack."[17] The definition (1) fails to demonstrate any link to centers of gravity, (2) does not provide for individuals or the full range of nonphysical entities (i.e., information) as potential decisive points, and (3) is inexplicably linked only to offensive operations (implying that there are no decisive points during defensive op-

---

[16] Rajiv Chandrasekaran, "Sunnis in Iraq Protest U.S. Occupation," *Washington Post*, April 19, 2003, p. A01.

[17] Joint Publication 1-02, *Department of Defense Dictionary of Military and Associated Terms*, Washington, D.C.: Joint Chiefs of Staff, April 12, 2001 (as amended through May 23, 2003), p. 144.

erations). Even if one does not accept that decisive points are most valuable when considered in conjunction with a center of gravity, point 2 ignores the reality of modern areas of operation. Point 3 fails not only in unnecessarily restricting the use of a potentially valuable concept to attack alone, but again, as in the case of center of gravity, appears to limit it to combat operations.

The authors propose a broader and hopefully more valuable construct: "A decisive point is a point that has value due to its potential influence in unbalancing or destabilizing a center of gravity."[18] In this context a "point" can be a piece of terrain, an individual, an element of physical or social infrastructure, an event, a function, or a less tangible factor such as a belief or predisposition.

The shortfalls in the current doctrinal conceptions of battle command, center of gravity, and decisive points are more evident in the light of urban operations' demands. Combat is seldom amenable to clean boundaries between its offensive and defensive components and related stability and support activities. The blurred line becomes a smear when the densities confronted in urban environments assert themselves. Battle command, as the concept is used in the following pages, will *include* the doctrinal "exercise of command in operations against a hostile, thinking enemy" without *limiting* itself to operations involving an enemy. Ultimately what is called for when commanders confront the challenges and complexity of today's urban environments is something much akin to the U.S. Army's mission command, i.e.,

> the conduct of military operations through decentralized execution based on mission orders for effective mission accomplishment. Successful mission command results from subordinate leaders at all echelons exercising disciplined initiative within the

---

[18] A fuller discussion of centers of gravity and decisive points appears in Glenn, *Managing Complexity During Urban Operations: Visualizing the Elephant.*

commander's intent to accomplish missions. It requires an environment of trust and mutual understanding.[19]

A British perspective on mission command is helpful in clarifying the essentials that underlie the approach. British doctrine considers mission command as a process with five elements:

- A commander gives his orders in a manner to ensure that his subordinates understand his intentions, their own missions, and the context of those missions.

- Subordinates are told what effect they are to achieve and the reason why it needs to be achieved.

- Subordinates are allocated the appropriate resources to carry out their missions.

- A commander uses a minimum of control measures so as not to limit unnecessarily the freedom of action of his subordinates.

- Subordinates then decide within their delegated freedom of action how best to achieve their missions.[20]

As with any aspect of command, applying mission command requires an understanding of the situation and the subordinates' capabilities. The demands for disciplined initiative and reliance on decentralized decisionmaking in the often highly politicized urban environment make extraordinary demands on military training and professionalism. It may be difficult to bring these many requirements together at the requisite time and place during an urban operation. As such, there may well be times when mission command is not the appropriate choice for exercising command.[21]

---

[19] Field Manual 6-0, *Mission Command: Command and Control of Army Forces,* Approved Final Draft, Washington, D.C.: Headquarters, Department of the Army, October 2002, p. 1-17.

Mission orders "are a technique for completing combat orders to allow subordinates maximum freedom of planning and action to accomplish missions that leave the 'how' of mission accomplishment to the subordinate" (see p. 1-18).

[20] R.A.M.S. Melvin, "Mission Command," *British Army Review*, Autumn 2002, pp. 4–5.

[21] Ibid., p. 5.

Battle Command and the Challenges of the Urban Environment

The number and density of elements inherent in any urban operation make it a difficult and complex undertaking. The following analysis employs the four components of command, control, ISR, and communications while providing a sampling of the aforementioned challenges a commander is likely to confront.

Command

LTG Harold G. Moore, commander at LZ (Landing Zone) X-Ray in November 1965 and co-author of the Vietnam classic *We Were Soldiers Once . . . and Young*, writes that "a commander in battle has three means of influencing the action: fire support . . . his personal presence on the battlefield, and the use of his reserve."[22] Urban areas conspire against all three of these. First, fire support is complicated by "dead space," those areas that are inaccessible to munitions because they are screened by an obstacle. Buildings, high-rises in particular, present a "shadow" such that a round fired from an artillery piece, aircraft, or other platform cannot strike a target within a given distance on the other side of the obstacle. Even aircraft have difficulties, despite their ability to adjust their angle of approach. Structures can interfere with laser designation or the trajectory of munitions after release, or an enemy may realize that there are a limited number of possible aircraft approaches and cover them with air defense weapons. Finally, rules of engagement can mean that some targets may not be engaged even when a weapon system can acquire the enemy. The proximity of innocents or friendly forces frequently rules out taking advantage of such situations. These many urban challenges call for the development of alternative fire support concepts to complement traditional approaches. Doctrine, including innovative control measures, and technologies are needed if a force is to be able to suppress, destroy, or meet other fire support tasks. These concepts would ideally encompass the employment of lethal and nonlethal means while

---

[22] Field Manual 6-0, p. 2-28.

incorporating civilian casualty, collateral damage, and other ROE issues as appropriate.[23]

A commander seeks to be at that spot on the battlefield where his presence is most needed. Determining the point of greatest need can be difficult to discern. As will be addressed in greater detail below, most military communications are line-of-sight, i.e., they require an unbroken path between a transmitter and receiver (though reflection and some other phenomena allow communications to occur without direct line-of-sight under some circumstances).[24] A commander therefore might not receive the timely communications he needs to determine where his presence is most in demand. Further, direct movement between two points on the urban battlefield is seldom possible even in a no-threat situation. Travel times and distances are lengthened by the need to stay on streets rather than go from one point to another "as the crow flies." The threat of enemy fire means that even longer routes are necessary to avoid falling prey to an ambush or passing through other enemy-held territory. Helicopter delivery seems a likely solution, but rotary-wing aircraft have proved notably vulnerable in urban environments, especially when hovering or landing.

Even use of the reserve is hindered. The same problems that plague a commander's responsiveness apply to committing a reserve. But now, rather than one vehicle or individual having to move, large numbers mean that routes of sufficient width to handle combat vehicles have to be found. The reserve has to select a way of getting to its desired point without undue loss from ground or air fires. That such challenges can be of consequence is clear when reading of Lieutenant Hollis's experiences in Mogadishu as described in the opening pages.

Command is further complicated by the heterogeneity of urban terrain, changes in operational tempo, and increased attrition of manpower and supplies, to touch on but a few factors. A commander

---

[23] The authors thank Gideon Avidor for this insight.

[24] For more on communications in urban environments, see Edwards, *Freeing Mercury's Wings: Improving Tactical Communications in Cities.*

wanting to secure a block of high-rise apartment buildings surrounded by a neighborhood of shorter structures has to determine how he will move the large number of assault forces called for into position while providing cover and concealment in the surrounding buildings. FM 3-06.11 suggests that a company normally attacks on a one- to two-block front in an urban area and a battalion on a two- to four-block front (based on city blocks averaging 175 meters wide). However, the manual also recognizes that the nature of the terrain and enemy will impact actual assignments.[25] Tempo measured as the amount of terrain taken per unit time might seem negligible when the commander follows the progress of an assault force as it moves floor-to-floor through the apartment complex (especially if he is following its progress on a two-dimensional map). Tempo in terms of activity per unit time at the point of the spear is at the same time frenetic. Costs in manpower and supplies will reflect that reality. The straight-line distance of a few tens of meters can take long minutes, even hours, to traverse should a commander desire to move himself or others from a unit on the sixth floor of one building to that in another structure. In brief, urban areas tend to hinder virtually every means a commander has to establish the conditions for success and then directly influence the operations conducted to achieve that success. They also challenge traditional ways of monitoring a unit's progress or measuring operational success. Time rather than distance covered or ground taken may be the primary measure of what constitutes success during planning and execution.[26] It may be the factor most critical in determining which course of action or type of unit is selected to accomplish a mission.

Additional demands make themselves known at the same time that the environment hinders execution of such "routine" command functions. Almost any of today's operations involve coalition members. Such cooperation inevitably comes with language, coordination,

---

[25] Field Manual 3-06.11, *Combined Arms Operations in Urban Terrain,* Washington, D.C.: Headquarters, Department of the Army, Chapter 4, Section IV, 14, February 28, 2002, p. 4.

[26] Gideon Avidor provided this comment during his formal review of the study.

logistics, and other concerns regardless of the environment. Seldom are so many different nations represented in so small a space as occurs in a city, however. And seldom is the character of support elsewhere such that U.S. forces are within small-arms range of another military's compound (as was the case in Mogadishu) or that they will rely on a coalition member for basic logistical or operational support (as experienced by the Americans in Mogadishu and Australian forces operating in Dili, East Timor).

Command is further complicated by the need to coordinate with local government officials or their representatives. The nature of the relationship between a U.S. commander and these individuals will depend on a number of factors (e.g., the level of hostilities, legitimacy of the indigenous government, and the capabilities of local law enforcement or other public services personnel). His proper limits of authority must be determined, disseminated, and exercised. He must have on hand the resources to meet the demands of his authority as well as other capabilities necessary to fulfill other missions. To the extent possible, U.S. military leaders leave the day-to-day operations of a built-up area to the in-place authorities. As Mogadishu, Haiti, and most recently the towns and cities in Iraq have demonstrated, these authorities may be incapable of assuming responsibility for public safety and good order.

Civil affairs, staff judge advocate, and chaplaincy personnel are invaluable in the assistance they provide in these several regards. They help not only in establishing and maintaining order, but also in educating the commander so that he communicates effectively, thereby best serving the interests of mission accomplishment. This assistance is by no means trivial. Understanding local society's power structures can mean the difference between coordinating with an individual who can truly assist in reducing the threat to a commander's soldiers and bargaining with one whose influence is limited or founded more on self-esteem than reality.

Control

Control is how the commander synchronizes his varied assets so that they support the common objective: mission accomplishment. A commander and his staff exert control through personal contact, plans, good training, instructions and orders passed via any effective medium, the commander's intent, and other means to get the word in a timely fashion to the force that needs it. Doctrinally, the U.S. Army defines control as

> the regulation of forces and other battlefield operating systems (BOS) to accomplish the mission in accordance with the commander's intent. It includes collecting, processing, displaying, storing, and disseminating relevant information for creating the common operational picture and using information during the operations process.[27]

The urban environment is no more favorable to control than it is to command. The same line-of-sight, difficulty of navigation, length of route, and other factors consort to interfere with a commander's ability to effectively direct his forces during operations in built-up areas. His inability to maintain consistent communications and assure that he is always properly positioned means that centralized oversight will be impossible. Even with better communications and mobility, the complexity of the urban environment means that the information he must sift through is so voluminous as to make it impossible to effectively control operations personally. The literature on urban operations is in general agreement that decentralization of authority is a fundamental characteristic of such endeavors. The men on the ground are best able to determine appropriate actions and adapt their guidance to best suit a commander's intent. A commander can most ably serve them and his own best interests by ensuring that his subordinate leaders are trained to make the kinds of decisions they will confront during urban operations by clearly articulating his intent and by giving those leaders the resources they need to accomplish assigned tasks. Urban areas will require that subordinate leaders lead and that their senior leaders prepare and allow them to do so. As General Krulak said, "the inescapable lessons of

---

[27] Field Manual 6-0, p. 1-13.

Somalia and other recent operations, whether humanitarian assistance, peacekeeping, or traditional warfighting, is that their outcome may hinge on the decisions made by small unit leaders and by actions taken at the *lowest* level."[28]

There is a contradiction of sorts to this guidance. Low-density assets such as medics and fire support officers (FSOs) may have to be managed in a more centralized manner than in more open environments. This is because the urban battlefield is so compartmented that it may take half an hour to retrace a route through buildings to return to a frontline unit only tens of meters away. The allocation of one medic per infantry platoon could well prove insufficient. Weighting a main effort or holding medics back at platoon command posts could prove to be more effective ways of providing support than decentralizing these too-rare assets.[29]

The commander will be responsible for controlling civilians more so in a city than in other environments. He will be able to employ force, the threat of force, negotiation, compromise, and cajoling to a greater or lesser extent depending on the condition of the indigenous government and the legal status of his own armed forces. It is not only his own forces that the commander may have to control. His authority will differ depending on the object of his efforts. Members of the local population might fall under his legal jurisdiction. His influence regarding members of the media, private volunteer, or nongovernmental organizations (NGOs) might be quite different in effect. Commanders should be knowledgeable with regard to their legal responsibilities and the extent of their authority before they are asked to command during an urban contingency. Improved training, to include challenging exercises with players representing noncombatant, media, NGO, and other relevant entities is called for.

---

[28] Charles C. Krulak, "The Strategic Corporal: Leadership in the Three Block War," *Marines Magazine*, January 1999, pp. 28–34.

[29] The issue of centralized control of combat service support and similarly low-density assets is more thoroughly discussed in Russell W. Glenn, Steven L. Hartman, and Scott Gerwehr, *Urban Combat Service Support Operations: The Shoulders of Atlas,* Santa Monica, CA: RAND Corporation, MR-1717-A, 2004.

The nature of civilian control tasks will differ considerably over time and space. The character of the control itself will therefore have to vary. A commander's resources will influence that character. Enforcing a curfew with plentiful manpower means that the area of concern can be saturated with patrols that detain or search anyone found in prohibited areas. More likely, curfew will be less a blanket condition than a demonstration of authority through the establishment of roadblocks and checkpoints or vehicle patrols. Those manning checkpoints may do little more than deny passage. In other situations they might stop vehicles and conduct searches, screen passengers and make arrests, organize convoys of civilian vehicles traveling under the supervision or protection of U.S. forces, or divert traffic to specified routes. Other tasks historically conducted in support of urban operations involving civilians include evacuation of personnel from all or part of a built-up area, supervision of forced labor teams, or disarming indigenous population members.[30] The extent of control permitted by each such option differs considerably. The differences in control can have both immediate and longer-term effects on urban stability.

ISR

Just as control is essential to effective command, so too are the functions of intelligence, surveillance, and reconnaissance necessary underpinnings for control of military operations. FM 6-0, *Mission Command,* notes that "the most important element of control is information; it is the most important C2 [command and control] resource available to the commander. Intelligence is an important and unique subset of information in C2."[31] While the difficulties inherent in command and control during urban operations are issues primarily of magnitude (e.g., there are more breaks in lines of sight; going from point A to point B takes longer), those regarding ISR tend to be more

---

[30] Regarding forced labor, the Geneva Accords prohibit the use of civilians in combat operations. However, they may be required to perform some forms of forced labor prior to and after the conduct of combat operations.

[31] Field Manual 6-0, p. 1-13.

substantive in nature. The ubiquity of concealment in urban environments, most generally in the form of man-made structures and civilian activities, means that many collection assets will play a less vital role here than elsewhere. Overhead imagery system designs seek to "see" what is below, whether through unrestricted line-of-sight or via technological means such as infrared or thermal capabilities that detect even with line-of-sight interruptions in visual wavelengths. Unmanned aerial vehicles (UAVs), satellites, and manned overhead reconnaissance assets will undeniably still aid in detecting, identifying, tracking, and targeting an enemy, but that enemy will quickly learn to avoid detection by keeping his military assets within structures and using civilian systems, e.g., trucks instead of armored personnel carriers. The urban foe, especially the defender familiar with the terrain, can employ existent telephone lines, military wire, cellular technology, couriers, and other means of communication to defeat friendly-force signals intelligence (SIGINT) efforts. The sheer volume of electromagnetic signals found in larger urban areas can make collection difficult—even if the foe employs standard military radios. There is therefore a need to employ systems of collection capabilities, e.g., overhead imagery to determine where to place observation posts.[32]

The density of radio frequency signals in an urban environment, emitted from commercial systems as well as wireless and paging systems, is yet another complicating factor. The adversary will also use existent power sources or tap into power lines to avoid the telltale visual and noise signatures associated with generators. Other traditional forms of intelligence collection are similarly stymied to a greater or lesser extent. For example, the foe's knowledge of local activities, including traffic patterns and gatherings, can be used to mask military movements and activities. The exception is in the human intelligence (HUMINT) realm. Military reconnaissance and surveillance units, owing to the likelihood of their being detected as well as

---

[32] Dan Caterinicchia, "Army considers urban warfare tech," *Federal Computer Week,* January 6, 2003, http://www.fcw.com/fcw/articles/2003/0106/web-cecom-01-06-03.asp, accessed June 25, 2003.

the restricted lines of sight, will be hindered. However, the density of civilians, many of whom will be amenable to assisting the friendly force either through good will or in return for some form of compensation, offers a rich source of intelligence. Unfortunately, this is the least reliable form of intelligence. Local civilians may pass on what they think friendly-force intelligence collectors want to hear rather than the truth, either in accord with their own cultural norms or under the assumption that such "kindness" will improve the payment received for information. Indigenous personnel may be under the control of the enemy or opposing factions and thus told to provide false or marginally valuable data. Intelligence personnel will therefore have to cultivate local sources carefully and attempt to obtain verification of the information they provide. This can be done by using redundant HUMINT assets to collect the same material; using initial HUMINT reports to key limited UAV, unmanned ground vehicle (UGV), SIGINT, or other capabilities; or a combination of these and additional means.

Finally, the nature of the intelligence sought during urban operations may differ fundamentally from that which dominates the collection process in other environments. Quantities (e.g., numbers of an opposing force or strength of an influence group) will sometimes matter far less than the influence an entity wields or the obstacles to mission accomplishment that it poses.[33] If the campaign objective is to facilitate fair elections and install the chosen government, for example, an opposition's ability to frustrate the process through disinformation, intimidation, or purchase of key support could be far more significant that the actual manpower strength of the potential troublemaker. In one way this is nothing new to the military analyst: capabilities rather than raw numbers have always been the base measure of a threat. The British at Rhorke's Drift and the coalition victory in the 2003 war in Iraq are examples in which the numbers far exceeded what the foe could do with them. But the likelihood that a force will have to deal with multiple types of challenge (e.g., force-on-

---

[33] The authors thank Gideon Avidor for this observation.

force combat, accurately informing the public, and coordinating security for media, private voluntary organiz

ations (PVO), and NGO representatives) and the ways that
threats can affect mission success may mean that capabilities are more
independent of raw numbers than is generally the case elsewhere. The
intelligence community has to some extent realized this: the templates
used during the intelligence preparation of the battlefield (IPB) process supporting urban actions are very much different in character than
the standard overlays of the Cold War. They frequently seek patterns
or record information with little connection to quantitative measures.
Yet amounts still dominate most intelligence analysts' approaches, a
mindset that could prove counterproductive.

Communications

Previously mentioned line-of-sight problems that disrupt communications can in some cases be overcome through the use of local communications means (e.g., local telephone systems). Similarly, savvy
communications personnel can make greater use of directional antennas, higher power settings on radios, or insightful location of primary and relay capabilities to reduce the negative consequences of
operating in a city. Often these workarounds will be of limited appli-
cability and benefit. Leaders will have to establish redundant means
of communications and train their subordinates to operate under
conditions in which their communications both within their units
and between organizations are subject to frequent interruption. Other
mechanisms key to command and control will also suffer. Global positioning systems (GPS), like radios, generally require uninterrupted
line-of-sight, so any system that relies on GPS for providing unit locations, targeting, or other purposes should be employed with awareness of the potential for interruptions. Required angles for successful
laser designation are sometimes unachievable given the presence of
structures and the flight profiles of ground-fired or air-released munitions. It may be that the most critical communication during an operation occurs when a commander tells his subordinates of his intent,
thereby allowing them to serve the interest of mission accomplish-

ment even in the absence of active man-to-man or system-to-system links.

Concluding Observations

Recent and emerging urban operations doctrine reflects an understanding of the above-mentioned challenges for command, control, ISR, and communications. Joint doctrine offers the five activities of understand, shape, engage, consolidate, and transition as a means to envision and execute urban undertakings.[34] U.S. Army doctrine suggests the use of four similar activities—assess, shape, dominate, and transition—for the same purpose.[35] The two sets are compatible. Commanders can employ one or the other based on personal preference or operational environment factors. The focus of this study is to find ways of overcoming the specific problems touched on above and the many more lying in wait for U.S. forces committed to urban actions given an understanding of these and other constructs. The next chapter expands on the nature and scope of the difficulties such undertakings entail and proposes possible solutions to better enable a leader to prepare his soldiers to successfully execute missions in this trying environment.

---

[34] Joint Publication 3-06, *Doctrine for Joint Urban Operations,* Washington, D.C.: Joint Chiefs of Staff, September 16, 2002, p. II-8.

[35] Field Manual 3-06, *Urban Operations,* Washington, D.C.: Headquarters, Department of the Army, June 2003, p. 5-1.

CHAPTER THREE

Challenges and Recommendations

Urban battle command makes exceptional demands on commanders at both the operational and tactical levels of war. We now consider the nature of these challenges for each element of battle command: command and leadership, control, ISR, and communications.

To lend continuity to the following discussions, this analysis employs seven general categories:

1. Look deeper in time and beyond military considerations during the backward planning process.
2. Consider second- and higher-order effects during planning and war gaming.
3. Doctrine asks lower-echelon leaders to look two levels up. Higher-echelon commanders need to consider the limits and perspectives of same nation and other subordinate headquarters and units. Commanders at every echelon need to be conscious of the situation as it impacts those at higher, lower, adjacent, joint, multinational, and interagency levels.
4. Account for the language, cultural, procedural, and other differences that will impede the tempo and level of understanding when dealing with some coalition member units and other agencies.
5. Be aware that urban densities compress the operational area and can result in more incidents of fratricide.
6. Get the ROE right as quickly as possible.
7. See the forest *and* selected trees.

With each new discussion we shall present a matrix that shows which of these issues are taken up for each element of battle command.

Command and Leadership During Urban Operations

We divide this discussion into the operational level and the tactical level.

The Operational Level of War

> In my day, as a junior leader, my decisions had an immediate impact on my troops and the enemy. In today's military operations the decisions of junior leaders still have those immediate impacts, but modern telecommunications can also magnify every incident, put every incident under a media microscope, and send descriptions and images of every incident instantly around the world for scores of experts and commentators to interpret for millions of viewers and listeners. Thus the decisions of junior leaders and the actions of their small teams can influence the course of international affairs.[1]
>
> Major General P. J. Cosgrove
> Australian Chief of Defence Forces

Actions in an urban area can themselves fundamentally comprise a military operation (e.g., Manila in 1945) or, more frequently, be a part of a larger operation (e.g., Baghdad, 2003). In either case it is important to realize that not all activities inherent in an urban operation are conducted within the built-up area itself. Cities are not independent entities. They rely on regional and in many cases national and international support. Hong Kong offers an interesting example in both regards. First, the very urbanized island of Hong Kong re-

---

[1] Alan Ryan, "Primary Responsibilities and Primary Risks," *Australian Defence Force Participation in the International Force East Timor,* Land Warfare Studies Centre Study Paper No. 304, November 2000, p. 84.

ceives its water from the mainland. The continued survival of the island's urbanization would be impossible without this outside supply. On a grander scale, the very existence of Hong Kong in its entirety is dependent on worldwide commerce. The city would not exist as more than perhaps a fishing village without the exchange between itself and the remainder of mainland China as well as the rest of the world.

The lesson for the military commander is straightforward. Activities at the operational level that focus merely on buildings and the people within the borders of a city will fail to capitalize on what can be gained in recognizing the urban area as part of a larger system. Taking this broader perspective will have implications during support operations (e.g., the metropolitan area will need the support of the region to thrive and, probably, vice versa). It will influence stability operations in which insurgents, criminals, terrorists, or other sources of problems are reliant on support from outside the city in question. It can also vitally influence the success of offensive or defensive operations. Isolation of a city, town, or village has always been a desirable first step during urban undertakings. This initial action is sometimes critical to keeping the enemy from escaping the built-up area to fight again. More often it is crucial to denying that foe access to reinforcements and resupply that would allow him to perpetuate his defense.

Urban endeavors will frequently make extraordinary demands on operational-level commanders. Activities at the operational level of war, that "at which campaigns and major operations are planned, conducted, and sustained to accomplish strategic objectives within theaters or areas of operations," are no less affected by urban complexity than are those at the tactical level.[2] Studying recent conflicts assists both in identifying how better to serve the strategic objectives sought and in determining the extent to which that complexity will complicate a commander's task. The analysis below considers several issues derived from a review of the immediate past and their implications for the future.

---

[2] Joint Publication 1-02, p. 324.

All categories are covered in this discussion.

The Operational Level of War

Look deeper in time and beyond military considerations during the backward planning process.	✔
Consider second- and higher-order effects during planning and war gaming.	✔
Doctrine asks lower-echelon leaders to look two levels up. Higher-echelon commanders need to consider the limits and perspectives of same nation and other subordinate headquarters and units. Commanders at every echelon need to be conscious of the situation as it impacts those at higher, lower, adjacent, joint, multinational, and interagency levels.	✔
Account for the language, cultural, procedural, and other differences that will impede the tempo and level of understanding when dealing with some coalition member units and other agencies.	✔
Be aware that urban densities compress the operational area and can result in more incidents of fratricide.	✔
Get the ROE right as quickly as possible.	✔
See the forest *and* selected trees.	✔

Look deeper in time and beyond military considerations during the backward planning process.

The traditional military "backward planning process" that has been adequate for addressing military objectives in the past is proving myopic when applied to the demands of more recent conflicts.[3] The shortfall is not in the process, however, but rather in the point selected from which to begin planning. Backward planning involves identifying a future event or point in time, normally referred to as the "desired end state." Planners then work from that future state back

---

[3] LTC Mike Chura, in looking at an early draft of this study, observed that emerging U.S. Army doctrine as articulated in drafts of FM 5-0 "will address backward planning as reverse planning, and that it is normally associated with time management at the lower tactical levels." The authors have chosen to retain the term "backward planning process" as (1) many readers are familiar with and have applied the concept and (2) the methods suggested here are applicable regardless of the level of war.

toward the present. Such a method has repeatedly proved effective in helping a commander determine how best to allocate his resources, especially that of time. The desired end state is generally defined in task-accomplishment terms, e.g., what the unit looks like after it has secured its terrain objective. The focus has been primarily, even exclusively, a military one. Such a procedure can result in plans that ultimately work against achieving strategic objectives. It would be better to take a longer and more comprehensive perspective when determining the end state from which to start. An appropriate operational-level starting place would be the point at which a command turns over responsibility for a city to an indigenous government or international stability force rather than, say, the point in time when the urban area is seized. By increasing the chronological scope (from the time of seizure through all subsequent actions until the city is turned over to another force or government), the commander forces himself to consider a broader scope of responsibilities, including exit strategies. Viewing a more distant desired end state should cause a commander and his staff to envision operations in terms of all relevant areas: military, political, social, economic, and diplomatic.

Targets that might be destroyed when only a military end state is considered are now neutralized in less destructive ways. Other facilities that will be valuable in helping the local population to more smoothly transition to postcombat stability might not only be spared but be actively protected. Such a perspective will be especially valuable in planning effective psychological operations. Rather than designing such operations simply to support immediate tactical needs, those requirements can be integrated with longer-term goals that will help to facilitate less conflict with civilians after fighting against an opposing military force has ceased.

Consider second- and higher-order effects during planning and war gaming.

A need to consider urban challenges from the perspective of greater breadth matches the requirement to look deeper in time. Virtually any military action has consequences beyond those immediately intended. Some are positive. Many are otherwise. Providing food and medical care to a town's civilians has the sought-after primary effect of reducing hunger and disease. A second-order effect might be an increased willingness by residents to provide intelligence on an enemy or criminal element. A negative second-order effect could be the ill will generated when the free distribution of aid ceases.

It is essential to determine second- and higher-order effects and incorporate that knowledge into plans and the conduct of military activities. The supplementary effects of military actions are in many cases more broadly and quickly felt in urban areas. The result can be what one doctrinal publication calls an "either intentional or unintentional . . . cascading effect . . . on the other elements of the urban infrastructure."[4] Destroying a bridge in a remote farming community means that a few wagonloads of goods do not get to market. The same action in a city can deprive thousands of power and water (if that bridge carried electrical lines and water pipes) or medical care (if doctors lived on the far side of the river). The increased density of civilians found in an urban area also presents opportunities. The effects of psychological operations (PSYOP) or deception can be more quickly registered in a metropolitan area due to the number of ways of communicating and the greater number of opportunities for individuals to pass information via personal contact. The discussion of "centers of gravity," "decisive points," and the need to determine other critical points has application here. Identifying such critical nodes is part of any good planning and execution. Understanding the relationships between the nodes and the effects of a given action on the system of nodes and relationships is also vital. Operational-level war games should include efforts to identify important nodes, how they are interrelated, what influence they could have on the accomplishment of friendly-force strategic objectives, and the immediate and higher-order effects of military actions on them.

Attempts to thoroughly analyze second- and higher-order effects could quickly overwhelm a decisionmaking process when the operational area includes an environment as complex as a modern city.

---

[4] Field Manual 3-20.96, *RSTA Squadron*, 2nd Coordinating Draft, Fort Knox, KY: U.S. Army Armor Center, undated, p. 3-26.

Commanders and staff leaders will have to prioritize these efforts, giving greater emphasis to the effects of greater consequence. For example, the strategic consequences of collateral damage to high-profile buildings adjacent to legitimate targets might mean that artillery planning requires detailed war gaming of effects. Fortunately, the increasing availability of precision munitions reduces the magnitude of such analyses to some extent, though a built-up area's density of people and structures means that the number of possible incidental losses from any single round could be high.[5] Determining acceptable risk will be a critical part of war gaming effects.

The concepts of "effects-based bombing" or "effects-based operations" will also help in this regard. The terms might be new; the logic behind them is hardly so:

> In one guise or another, effects-based operations have always been with us. They are what good generals, admirals, and statesmen have always tried to do: to focus on shaping the adversary's thinking and behavior rather than on simply defeating his forces. They are close to the heart of the writings of Sun Tzu and of Clausewitz on military operations. Moreover, as the allusion to military and political leaders indicates, effects-based operations are neither simply a mode of tactical level warfare, nor peculiarly military in nature. They also encompass the full range of political, economic, and military actions that a nation might want to take to shape the behavior of an enemy, a would-be opponent, and even of allies and neutrals. These actions may include destruction of an enemy's forces and capabilities, that is, attrition-based operations. However, the objective of an effects-based strategy and of those actions that advance it is not simply to destroy physical capabilities, but to induce an opponent, neutral, or ally to pursue a course of action in keeping with our interests.[6]

---

[5] Anthony H. Cordesman, *The "Instant Lessons" of the Iraq War: Main Report,* Third Working Draft, Washington, D.C.: Center for Strategic and International Studies, April 14, 2003, p. 10.

[6] Edward A. Smith, Jr., *Effects Based Operations: Applying Network Centric Warfare in Peace, Crisis and War,* Washington, D.C.: CCRP Publication Series, 2002, p. 103.

The focus is not on the extent of damage created by an operation, but rather the effect desired.[7] Thus, if a commander wants to prevent an adversary's crossing a river, he might mine the far shore or otherwise block all approaches to the bank rather than destroy the bridge crossing it. Yet, again, there will be a need to look beyond only the primary level of analysis. Obviously the presence of noncombatants and their vulnerability to injury might influence the means used to deny the enemy access to crossing points, as would the friendly force's obstacle-clearing capabilities that would be needed were it to cross and have to clear its own barriers. Effects-based considerations need to contemplate more than only those units involved in planning at the current time and place. For our example here, the important factor would be the obstacle-clearing capabilities of a friendly unit likely to be tasked with the crossing mission, not those of the unit currently defending. Similarly, those performing air targeting might specify precisely what part of an electrical power facility to strike, to allow its postcombat rapid repair. If that facility is potentially an alternate target for other air units, they too must be informed of the constraints on their attack. The capabilities to support such precision air-to-ground engagements, even short-notice missions involving close air support, have dramatically improved in recent years. The Litening II precision attack targeting system, for example, is highly regarded for what it offers B-52 and other fixed-wing aircraft in the way of much-improved detection, acquisition, tracking, and target-identification capabilities.[8]

The potential effects go beyond physical effects alone. Indeed, Smith argues that the key distinction between attrition-based warfare and effects-based warfare is that while the former is focused on physical targets and quantifiable results, the latter is focused on actions and

---

[7] Cordesman, *The "Instant Lessons" of the Iraq War: Main Report,* Third Working Draft, p. 10. Cordesman refers only to "effects-based bombing in this analysis."

[8] For a description of the Litening II system, see "More Bombs on Target: Laser targeting pod improves B-52 precision-strike capability," *Citizen Airman,* June 2003; and Robert Wall, "Litening Strikes: As combat operations in Iraq wind down, B-52/Litening combo makes debut," *Aviation Week & Space Technology,* April 28, 2003, p. 35.

will.[9] He identifies six primary effects, two physical, one (chaos/entropy) that can be either physical or psychological, and three psychological. These are destruction, physical attrition (destruction of multiple capabilities), chaos/entropy, foreclosure (cutting off potential courses of action), shock (sudden collapse of will), and psychological attrition (gradual erosion of will).[10]

War gaming that considers higher-order effects will include analysis of how military actions will be perceived by parties that might significantly influence operational or strategic success. This analysis must extend beyond parties imminently involved in a conflict to also consider long-term implications for national alliances, trade, and other social, political, and economic considerations. Choosing to guard the oil ministry building in Baghdad most likely makes considerable sense from the perspective of wanting to help the Iraqi people quickly reestablish a viable economy. However, given that much of the world believes that exploitation of Iraq's petroleum resources was a primary reason for coalition military operations, explaining the logic of the action or balancing it by also providing security for cultural, religious, or other facilities would have been well advised.

Doctrine asks lower-echelon leaders to look two levels up. Higher-echelon commanders need to consider the limits and perspectives of same nation (and other) subordinate headquarters and units.

The lower the echelon, the more limited a headquarters' capabilities. It is difficult for any staff below brigade level to approximate a thorough IPB process during active operations. It simply lacks the manpower and expertise to do so. This is true at any given time of day but is notably true from the perspective of having to maintain continuous operations; the lower the echelon, the less likely it is to be adequately manned for fully effective 24-hour activity.[11] Subordinate

---

[9] Smith, *Effects Based Operations: Applying Network Centric Warfare in Peace, Crisis and War,* p. 43.

[10] Ibid., pp. 257–265.

[11] David Potts (ed.), *The Big Issue: Command and Combat in the Information Age,* The Strategic and Combat Studies Institute Occasional Paper Number 45, March 2002, p. 62.

echelons likewise have less in the way of information-processing capabilities; the higher headquarters that pushes too much intelligence or other information downward punishes rather than assists its units. Alberts and Hayes suggest that information should, in fact, not be pushed either up or down the chain of command, but rather be posted and accessed via smart retrieval mechanisms.[12] (However, this does not ensure that headquarters personnel will be aware of the information's existence nor that they have the means to process and disseminate it after retrieval.) Based on an analysis of historical operations, they identify six levels of centralization of command and argue that the desired degree of centralization of command depends on a variety of factors, including communications availability, information availability and the degree of flexibility required, and the expertise and capability of subordinate forces. In general, command should be more centralized when these factors are low and less centralized when they are high. In the case of urban commanders, communications availability may be intermittent and information availability relatively low, while flexibility may be required. This suggests the suitability of an intermediate (or adaptable) level of centralization.

More robust command and control nodes need to either assume some of the processing burden on behalf of lower echelons or allocate tasks across those entities to not overburden any one too greatly. Information has to be screened based on the attributes of value and quality.[13] Leaders at any level need only see information of value to them. The higher the quality of that information the better (and the higher the priority that should be placed on getting it to those who will value it). However, the value of information depends in part upon the other information available. Information that supports existing plans or confirms existing information may be of less value than "new" information that questions the validity of plans or infor-

---

[12] David S. Alberts and Richard E. Hayes, *Power to the Edge: Command and Control in the Information Age*, Washington, D.C.: CCRP Publication Series, 2003.

[13] Richard Darilek, Walt L. Perry, Jerome Bracken, John Gordon, and Brian Nichiporuk, *Measures of Effectiveness for the Information-Age Army*, Santa Monica, CA: RAND Corporation, MR-1155-A, 2001, p. 9 (as quoted in Melvin, "Mission Command," p. 7).

mation.[14] "See first" is the initial of four future force warfighting concepts. The remaining three ("understand first," "act first," and "finish decisively") depend not on the receipt of intelligence, but rather on a headquarters (1) having a need for it, (2) being able to process it, and (3) receiving it in usable form in a timely manner. Only then will the benefit of seeing first provide an operational advantage.

Account for the language, cultural, procedural, and other differences that will impede the tempo and level of understanding when dealing with some coalition member units and other agencies.

Operational tempo will be affected by communications and cultural differences between coalition members. It may also be influenced by command arrangements. John Allison noted that "in the NATO alliance everyone gets a vote and a cut at it. By the time they figured out what to strike, [targets in Kosovo] were gone."[15] The normal 1/3–2/3 rule that requires a higher headquarters to provide two-thirds of available planning time to subordinate units may prove inadequate when in coalition environments. The Allied Command Europe Rapid Reaction Corps (AARC) has recently moved to a 1/4–3/4 approach.[16] Better are senior headquarters staff members that keep those at subordinate echelons informed of planning progress and key commander decisions. Planning at these lower levels can then proceed simultaneously with that above to minimize the time needed to complete an order or plan after receipt of the higher headquarters product.

Communications require a sender, a message, and a receiver. Successful communication of information requires clear articulation by the sender so that the receiver properly understands the message,

---

[14] For more information on this concept, see either Carl Builder, *Command Concepts: A Theory Derived from the Practice of Command and Control*, Santa Monica, CA: RAND Corporation, MR-775-OSD, 1999; or Darren J. Reid and Ralph E. Giffin, *A Woven Web of Guesses, Canto Three: Network Centric Warfare and the Virtuous Revolution*, International Command and Control Research and Technology Symposium, Washington, D.C.: CCRP, 2003.

[15] Allison, interview with Kingston, June 6, 2003.

[16] Potts, *The Big Issue*, p. 37.

and this passage must be fully completed in a timely manner. At present, language, experience level, and difficulties in information processing can too greatly impede comprehension and slow transmission. Technologies that assist in overcoming cultural barriers to understanding and speed staff processes can help, as can staffs and leaders more sensitive to demographic barriers that interfere with successful creation and receipt of messages.

Simply giving lower-level headquarters more time (or saving them time) is not always sufficient. Orders and briefings should avoid unnecessary nation- or service-specific verbiage. Visual design aids should aim at communicating effectively to all in the audience (an oft-forgotten objective during "PowerPoint wars" when competing staff sections attempt to outduel their counterparts in effects to most impress). Alan Ryan, a Research Fellow at the Australian Land Warfare Studies Centre, reported coalition member observations by those with the multinational International Force East Timor (INTERFET) headquarters headed by his nation during operations in East Timor that highlight the difficulties. They include comments by three Thai colonels who expressed concern that language was a problem to the extent that "Asian officers, in particular, understood only half of what was said at briefings and conferences, and they believed that Australian officers giving briefings appeared unaware of the issue." In particular, the speed with which briefings were concluded was problematic, as it left little time for requests for clarification or even for non-English speakers to formulate their queries.[17]

The difficulties extend to differences in training as well as language and procedures. Additionally, then Lieutenant Colonel Paul Eaton, Army Forces Somalia G3 during operations in Somalia, noted that the training levels of some coalition members introduces serious capability gaps. This is notably true with respect to units coming into theater to replace a country's original force (which are often the best a military has to offer in efforts to make a positive first impression). Kuwaiti ground forces came into theater with weapons that had never

---

[17] Ryan, "Primary Responsibilities," p. 92.

been fired. Representatives of other armies assisted them in setting up firing ranges.[18]

The additional complexity inherent in urban operations means that routine tasks will sometimes take considerably longer even when the parties involved are from the same country. One day was found to be insufficient for a relief-in-place involving a U.S. Army and Marine unit in Baghdad. The incoming unit later observed that "the relief in place with the Marines was conducted more hastily than necessary resulting in insufficient initial awareness of the contacts and contracts they had developed."[19] Obviously, the greater number of issues requiring resolution and differences in procedures and language will make such actions even more time consuming when they involve militaries from more than one nation.

John Allison believes that liaison officers (LNOs), sometimes also called language officers, are vitally important:

> LNO is a problem . . . you need a lot of them. Nobody has tables of organizations with ten LNOs . . . . He can bridge gaps and can report back to his organization . . . . The LNO builds relationships and rapport. You can't underestimate the value of relationships . . . . In command and control at the end of the day, that is what it gets down to . . . .
>
> [I] had a Pakistani in [the] headquarters when [UNOSOM II units were] moving out of Somalia. [Pakistanis] were going back in line. The Somalis were shooting, shooting up in the air . . . . There were reports that the Pakistanis were taking fire. It got almost up to the White House. I had a satellite call . . . I was able to say that no, we weren't taking fire, nobody was taking

---

[18] Harold E. Bullock, *Peace by Committee: Command and Control Issues in Multinational Peace Enforcement Operations*, thesis, Maxwell Air Force Base, AL: School of Advanced Airpower Studies, June 1994, p. 40.

[19] Ralph Hammond, "Operation Iraqi Freedom, Task Force 2-7 Infantry (Mechanized) After Action Review," Fort Benning, GA: Combined Arms and Tactics Directorate, U.S. Infantry School, undated.

fire . . . . The Pakistani LNO there had already contacted [the Pakistanis].[20]

Allison's remark that "nobody has tables of organizations with ten LNOs" notwithstanding, LTC Michael F. Chura, who was key in the development of both the U.S. Army's urban warfare and stability operations doctrine (FM 3-06 and 3-07, respectively), coincidentally notes that "in the world of stability operations, multiply the LNO requirements by a factor of 10!"[21] Even that number may be conservative for some units given the need to orchestrate the actions of same service, joint, multinational, other governmental, PVO, NGO, local government, and other organizations during urban operations.

Further problems arose in East Timor when various nations provided resources to other coalition nations. Some nations took what, as Ryan recorded, "appeared to be an inappropriately legalistic approach" to providing mutual support. Selected countries wanted to pay cash at the time a service (e.g., provision of fuel for a vehicle) was rendered.[22] Another took accountability to the extreme of charging a second for the water consumed by its liaison officer.[23] The INTERFET commander, General Cosgrove, noted similar difficulties in dealing with the United Nations bureaucracy during the transition phase, concluding that they should not be allowed to interfere with the mission. Rather, "future mission commanders [are advised] 'not to waste one joule of energy trying to change this bureaucracy in any material way but to understand and facilitate it both in the mission area and as appropriate in New York.'"[24]

Other challenges exist in dealing with PVOs, NGOs, and U.S. domestic agencies. Providing security for humanitarian relief flights in Somalia was complicated by the International Committee of the

---

[20] Allison, interview with Kingston, June 6, 2003.

[21] Michael F. Chura, "Some Thoughts on Urban Battle Command in the Twenty-First Century," email to Dr. Russell W. Glenn, December 15, 2003.

[22] Ryan, "Primary Responsibilities," p. 104.

[23] Ibid., p. 106.

[24] Ibid., p. 112.

Red Cross (ICRC) not allowing weapons on aircraft carrying such supplies.[25] Differences in levels of discipline and procedures could create situations in which members of one organization put others at risk. Some members of at least one emergency services department refused to wear respirators during the post September 11, 2001 cleanup of the World Trade Center site. Similar lapses during other urban undertakings could result in such personnel collapsing and requiring evacuation by others or other failures that put better-disciplined personnel in unnecessary danger. Military commanders need to be aware of these potential differences so that they can appropriately manage the involvement of other agencies and develop training requirements and contingency plans.

Be aware that urban densities compress the operational area and can result in more incidents of fratricide.

Density affects the proximity of friendly forces. Fratricide is an ever-present concern simply because more coalition elements (both U.S. and other) are crammed into less space. Urban navigation is tough even with good maps and GPS, first because the accuracy of GPS is limited, and second because the accuracy of the maps may be limited. The National Imagery Mapping Agency (NIMA) has lower accuracy standards for urban maps than other regions because of the difficulty in representing the density of urban structures. For example, when representing narrow roads and alleys, mapmakers sometimes need to distort their absolute locations and the representations of other nearby features. British troops use images rather than maps because of this problem. They locate the correct image using a higher-level grid reference and then identify their position both on the map and with GPS. Navigation then occurs using both the map and the GPS.[26]

---

[25] Joseph P. Hoar, "A CINC's Perspective," *Joint Forces Quarterly*, Autumn 1993, p. 57.

[26] Material in this paragraph is taken from Doug Ridenour and Jared L. Ware, interview with Gina Kingston, Arlington, Virginia, June 4, 2003. A reviewer within the U.S. Army G37 Battle Command staff section further notes that U.S. forces in JTF 190 used this technique in Port-au-Prince in 1994 when the 1:50000 maps were found unsuitable for stability and support operations.

Representatives of other militaries are less likely to be well-endowed in this regard than are American and British soldiers or marines, thus increasing the chances of unintentional contact. The compression of battlefield space also means that special operations forces may be in closer proximity to regular units. Given that the special operators (as well as many of the enemy) might be in civilian clothes, the threat of blue-on-blue engagements, which could include calling in fire support on friendly positions unknown to those at the tactical level, is higher in towns and cities than elsewhere.

Get the ROE right as quickly as possible.

Rules of engagement (ROE) dramatically affect the individual soldier or marine, sailor or airman, for it is they whose lives are at risk in an area of operations. ROE can also directly impact strategic success. Progress made during weeks of negotiation or months of psychological operations can be threatened by an ill-advised military action that kills or wounds an innocent noncombatant. It is difficult to provide individuals on (or over) the ground with sufficiently definitive yet flexible guidance while also doing what is feasible with respect to safeguarding noncombatant lives and property. The complexity of the situation from the combatant's perspective is summarized by Colonel Lee Gore, aviation brigade commander during Mogadishu operations in 1993. In the soldiers' view, it was a matter of "Who are you going to shoot at? Are you going to shoot only at those that shoot at you? If so you're just waiting around to be shot at. You don't know who's the bad guy. They all look the same."[27]

Initial ROE have too often been based on wishful thinking or initial misestimates that can cost unnecessary loss of friendly-force lives. Guidance given to soldiers in 1945 Manila and arguably in 1968 Hue qualifies in this regard. U.S. military leaders, during the latter, respected the request from the corps commander of the Army of the Republic of Vietnam (ARVN) to impose strict ROE on the use of fire support in hopes of saving the historic city and preventing needless civilian casualties. However, the ARVN commanders fight-

---

[27] Lee Gore interview, with Russell W. Glenn, Atlanta, Georgia, April 2, 2003.

ing in the oldest and most historic parts of the city were themselves calling in air strikes in support of their operations. American ROE were later made less restrictive (as happened in Manila after original restrictions on the use of artillery interfered with the success of tactical actions).[28]

On the other hand, what seems overly restrictive from the individual level may be apropos in the "bigger picture." Lieutenant Colonel Johnny Brooks recalled from his tenure as battalion commander during the 1989 Operation Just Cause that "you have to significantly worry about civilians. You have to worry about rules of engagement. We weren't allowed to use indirect fires, and it's good we weren't . . . We would have burned the town [of Colón] down."[29] The question is not how to get the ROE right; that will come with fine tuning once an operation begins. The challenge is to get the ROE close to right *before* operations start and thereafter adapt them quickly and effectively as necessary. That should involve a rigorous analytic process no less detailed, comprehensive, and flexible than the command estimate process. It should include war gaming, a process that would incorporate not only representatives playing the roles of friendly force and host nation government, but also various noncombatant groups, media, international and regional public opinion, and others as pertinent. To the authors' knowledge there is no study that investigates past efforts at creating ROE with the intention of providing a historical basis and procedure for "getting it close to right" the first time. Providing such an analysis would be valuable.

See the forest *and* selected trees.

The sheer volume of mission-relevant components in even a small city can be overwhelming. To use the quickly-becoming-trite but descriptive phrase, cities are truly systems of systems. As such, a commander needs to be able to see both the whole (to understand how its parts are interrelated) and selected individual parts (for he will inevitably lack sufficient resources to address the entirety all at once,

---

[28] Cooling, *Shaping the Battlespace*, p. 35.

[29] Johnny Brooks, interview with Russell W. Glenn, Fort Benning, Georgia, April 4, 2003.

and thus must know the most relevant of its parts). Both demand what Clausewitz called *coup d'oeil* and what current doctrine attempts to replicate through the concept of "visualization." *Coup d'oeil* is

> an intellect that, even in the darkest hour, retains some glimmerings of the inner light which leads to truth . . . . The concept merely refers to the quick recognition of a truth that the mind would ordinarily miss or would perceive only after long study and reflection . . . . It really is the commander's . . . ability to see things simply, to identify the whole business of war completely. . . . Only if the mind works in this comprehensive fashion can it achieve the freedom it needs to dominate events and not be dominated by them.[30]

FM 6-0 proposes the following definition for a commander's visualization:

> The mental process of achieving a clear understanding of the force's current state with relation to the enemy and environment (situational understanding), developing a desired end state which represents mission accomplishment, and then subsequently determining the key tasks involved in moving the force from its current state to the end state.[31]

The draft *Battle Command: Leadership and Decision Making for War and Operations Other Than War*, alternatively offers that "visualization is the act of forming a mental picture of the current and future state based on higher commanders' intent, available information, and intuition."[32]

All of these are more or less eloquent attempts to articulate that the commander needs to maintain an ability to understand the situation from both the macro and micro perspectives while not being

---

[30] Carl von Clausewitz, *On War*, Princeton: Princeton University Press, 1976, pp. 102 and 578.

[31] Field Manual 6-0, p. Glossary-2.

[32] *Battle Command: Leadership and Decision Making for War and Operations Other Than War*, Draft 2.1, Fort Leavenworth, KS: Battle Command Battle Laboratory, April 22, 1994, p. 13.

overwhelmed by the deluge of ongoing events. Perhaps Rudyard Kipling put it most articulately: the commander needs to be the man who can "keep your head when all about you are losing theirs."[33]

The already mentioned concepts of center of gravity and decisive points are key in this regard. The commander has to have some understanding of the whole if he is to identify critical nodes and understand their interworkings. His goal is to then determine how these individual "trees" in the forest of buildings, infrastructures, and social interactions can be influenced to best aid in the accomplishment of his mission. The complexity of the urban area will threaten to overwhelm the commander and his staff lacking the experience and intelligence to understand both the whole and its critical components. They need to be given the training and experience to understand what nodes are mission-relevant, which may be so in the future, how the commander can influence them, and their relationship to each other.

Having identified and discussed the seven categories used to frame our discussion at the operational level, the next section considers the impact each has on command and leadership at the tactical level.

The Tactical Level of War

> This acting without orders, in anticipation of orders, or without waiting for approval, yet always within the over-all intention, must become second nature in any form of warfare where formations do not fight en cadre, and must go down to the smallest units.
>
> Field Marshal Sir William Slim
> *Defeat into Victory*, 1961

---

[33] Rudyard Kipling, "If," http://stellar-one.com/poems/if__rudyard_kipling.htm, accessed June 16, 2003.

The Mogadishu experiences of Lieutenant Hollis depict the difficulties of leading even at the lowest echelons during urban operations. His experiences are substantiated by U.S. Army lessons learned, which conclude that the "biggest impediment to C2 is noise, incoming and outgoing" and recommend that units conduct "extensive live fire exercises" in order to acclimatize units to such conditions.[34] "Adapt" is probably better than "acclimatize" in describing what units and their commanders need to do. No matter how used to the noise a unit might become, its members will still have to find ways to communicate other than voice, radio, or other sound-based means during periods of intense combat. Adaptation will be similarly essential if leaders are to maintain accountability in what is probably the most compartmented of environments.

Tactical commanders at higher levels will sometimes share these problems and confront others as well. Company commanders in Hue during the fighting of Tet in 1968 struggled with guidance from echelons above that simply did not understand the conditions confronting marines on the streets. Even "perfect situational awareness" will not replicate the difficulty of close-quarters fighting or the situation as seen by those at the sharp end. Location monitors might provide accurate locations, but they probably will not show that squad members are separated by walls, in different rooms, or even on different floors. Video images cannot replicate the danger felt as rounds hit nearby walls or demonstrators rush a group of soldiers. At least in the near term, and probably for a considerable period beyond, units that train to operate in a decentralized manner within the bounds of the commander's intent will be the best prepared to handle the challenges of urban contingencies.

The following categories are covered in this discussion. Including the first two would be unnecessarily repetitive, as the differences between their operational and tactical application are fairly straightforward.

---

[34] "Urban Operation Lessons Learned TTPs," briefing, no organization specified, undated, http://www.infantry.army.mil/catd/urban_ops/, accessed April 20, 2003.

The Tactical Level of War

Look deeper in time and beyond military considerations during the backward planning process.	
Consider second- and higher-order effects during planning and war gaming.	
Doctrine asks lower-echelon leaders to look two levels up. Higher-echelon commanders need to consider the limits and perspectives of same nation and other subordinate headquarters and units. Commanders at every echelon need to be conscious of the situation as it impacts those at higher, lower, adjacent, joint, multinational, and interagency levels.	✔
Account for the language, cultural, procedural, and other differences that will impede the tempo and level of understanding when dealing with some coalition member units and other agencies.	✔
Be aware that urban densities compress the operational area and can result in more incidents of fratricide.	✔
Get the ROE right as quickly as possible.	✔
See the forest *and* selected trees.	✔

Doctrine asks lower-echelon leaders to look two levels up. Higher-echelon commanders need to consider the limits of same nation (and other) subordinate headquarters and units.

Operations in an urban environment have higher densities not only in terms of the *number of items per unit space*, but also with respect to the *quantity of activities per unit time*. The former will vary somewhat depending on the time of day, day of the week, or period of the year (e.g., there will be more cars on the road during working hours and typically more people in the city's main square on market day). There will be extremes of very low tempo during some periods and frenetic civilian activity at others. FM 3-0 states that "tempo is the rate of military action" and that "controlling or altering that rate is necessary to retain the initiative."[35] However, the latent tempo of nonmilitary activity in an urban area will more often than not be largely beyond the control of a military commander. That does not

---

[35] Field Manual 3-0, p. 5-12.

mean he should not attempt to influence it in ways favorable to mission accomplishment, but chances are that his resources will allow to affect selected aspects of tempo in only a limited area (e.g., via the imposition of martial law or actions aimed at reducing the amount of criminal activity in a particular neighborhood). The high tempo of both everyday activity and urban military operations means that plans and command styles have to allow the flexibility to adjust to this dynamic environment.

An effect of high-tempo operations in a spatially dense environment is potentially faster adaptation. Lieutenant Colonel Lee Gore experienced this firsthand as aviation task force commander in 1993 Mogadishu. Gore recalled that the adversary "adjusted to helicopter operations very quickly. They knew if they just waited in a street with [a rocket-propelled grenade] that eventually we would fly over and they would fire a rocket straight up into the belly . . . . You [had] to keep flight profiles very flexible. Otherwise after two or three times they learned what you were going to do and they'd just wait for you."[36]

Lieutenant Hollis's difficulties in leading his unit during the rush to aid soldiers in need were compounded by his problems with navigating Mogadishu's streets. High-tempo operations complicate matters in other ways as well. Calling for fire support or locating an aircraft flying overhead can become a near-impossible task if buildings block line-of-sight, even if one accurately and precisely knows his location. Colonel Gore recalled that during his combat experiences in Mogadishu,

> it was near impossible for a guy on the ground to ask for fire support and know where he wanted us to fire . . . . It's the gray building . . . . The two-story . . . . The one to the east ("What is your position?") . . . . We're firing tracers at it. ("We can't see the tracer in the day time.") . . . . As soon as they used smoke, it was drifting. It would stay in the adobe buildings. The desert environment was dusty all the time, and there was other smoke. Every time you hit a building with a rocket it powdered and

---

[36] Gore interview.

made a dust . . . . And you're trying to fly the aircraft at the same time he's calling for fire. We're trying to figure out which way is north, south, east, or west . . . . Ground forces may or may not follow schemes of maneuver. We've got to know what they are going to do before we go up in the air. What their objective is . . . . That's down to every pilot . . . . When they start getting dispersed all over a city, we don't have a clue where they are . . . . It just wasn't easy.[37]

Gore's experiences were by no means unique. Israeli infantry in 1973 Suez City called for supporting artillery fires but could not see the rounds impact because the soldiers were inside buildings with the enemy in very close proximity.[38] U.S. experiences in Grenada were even more sobering when an Air-Ground Liaison Officer attempted to kill a sniper via aviation fires:

The chief tried to call in a Spectre gunship but was told none was available. He was convinced of the need to act, so he made contact with the flight leader of four A-7s that had been busy over Calivigny. Although the chief did not know that brigade headquarters had moved (nor did the infantry battalions), he was certain of Raines' position, and Crocker used smoke to indicate his. It did not seem to be a difficult mission. The target was a white house with a red roof, on the ridge north of a drive-in movie. He described it to the pilot, giving him a bearing of 270 degrees from the Sugar Mill.

The leading A-7 came in very low, under 200 feet, for no fewer than three passes. As the aircraft flew over the target, the chief called "mark on top," indicating that he had located the house. The pilot seemed happy and told his wing man that the flight was active but not to fire until he did.

The aircraft came in low and fast. To the consternation of the chief and Stephens, they did not seem to be on the correct bearing, and as they drew near, the pilot was heard to say over

---

[37] Gore interview.

[38] BG (IDF, ret.) Nachum Zaken, Battalion Commander, 433 Armored Battalion, Armored Brigade #500 during 1973 fighting in Suez City, interview with Russell W. Glenn, Latrun, Israel, April 10, 2000.

his radio that he could see people near the house. This did not fit with the actual target. The chief yelled to abort the mission a second or so before the leading aircraft opened up with his 20-mm cannon—too late to stop a stream of shells ripping into Silvasy's new command post.

The pilot had fired into a gray building west of the drive-in movie, causing chaos and seventeen casualties, three of them serious. The worst was Sergeant Sean Luketina, a radio operator from the 82d's signal battalion, who had both legs smashed. Medical evacuation to the *Guam* was delayed, supposedly by a rain squall. Luketina later died of gangrene in his legs at the Walter Reed Hospital in the United States.[39]

Such difficulties are very likely not evident to a commander flying overhead, in his command post, or with another unit even a block or two away. Subordinate leaders on site, whether on the ground or in the air, need to have the authority to alter routes and plans to meet the challenges of the volatile environment. They will find solutions given the chance. In Gore's case, pilots conceived of using hand-held lasers for navigation and targeting. Pilots employed the lasers to point the way as army personnel worked their way through twisting Mogadishu streets. Either aviators would put a laser dot on a potential target (especially easy to see if those on the ground had night-vision goggles (NVGs) and it was night) or soldiers below would designate. At times both used a laser in a designation-confirmation mode: an infantry leader would put a spot on the target; the pilot would do the same for verification. Colonel Gore's helicopter crews facilitated such procedures by fastening their lasers directly to their aircraft's 20mm gun and running a piece of electrical wire into the cockpit.[40]

Commanders need to ensure that they properly resource their junior leaders in addition to granting subordinates the authority to make decisions independently. Resources encompass more than materiel. More frequent rotation of units may be necessary due to losses

---

[39] Mark Adkin, *Urgent Fury: The Battle for Grenada,* London: Leo Cooper, 1989, pp. 286–87.

[40] Gore interview.

in killed, wounded, or the increasing stress felt by those in contact with the enemy. There is evidence that urban operations are in general more stress-inducing than those in other environments. John Allison is one of many who are convinced that this is the case:

> I've told this to people before—and you're talking to a guy who got shot in the Gulf War [1991]—I never felt comfortable in the L.A. environment or Mogadishu. You always felt there was something that could get you killed. It could be the 9-year-old kid. You had a better feeling of control in Iraq knowing the bad guys were in front of us and the good guys were around me. We always knew what we had to do and we had tools at our disposal. In the Gulf we were not targets, we were moving forward. In L.A. we were trying to take control—and around any corner you don't know what's coming. You can't discern the good guys from the bad guys from the neutral guys which makes the stress, in my opinion, go up.[41]

Leaders need to be aware of the possible increased incidence of stress reaction. Having chaplains visit units frequently can be a significant help in this regard.[42] Likewise, providing access to other low-density assets such as military lawyers gives lower-level commanders a ready means of obtaining answers to the difficult questions that ROE, the presence of civilians, and other urban conditions can impose. Finally, urban hand-over procedures should be developed, added to tactical doctrine, and practiced in training before units deploy to urban areas. The types and quantity of information needed for effective hand-over could differ considerably between urban and other environments. Given the possibility that the transition from one unit to another might be driven by pending exhaustion, simply adding more to hand-over procedures is not the solution.

---

[41] John Allison, interview with Todd Helmus, Arlington, Virginia, June 5, 2003. LTC Allison was deployed to both the 1992 Los Angeles riots and Mogadishu, Somalia in addition to other tours of duty. Dr. Helmus and Dr. Glenn will publish a study on urban combat stress reaction in 2004.

[42] Field Manual 3-06, p. 9-24.

Account for the language, cultural, procedural, and other differences that will impede the tempo and level of understanding when dealing with some coalition member units and other agencies.

As Lieutenant Hollis noted, learning how to open the hatch on a coalition member's armored personnel carrier (APC) just as one prepares to move into combat is not the preferable state of affairs. Unfamiliarity with equipment can also plague soldiers in the same army. American light infantry soldiers from the 10th Mountain Division had not trained with M1 Abrams tanks before LTC Bob Clark's tank-infantry fighting vehicle (IFV) task force reached Somalia from Fort Stewart immediately after the events of October 3–4, 1993. Some in the M1 Abrams tanks and M2 Bradley IFVs had likewise never trained with a light infantry unit. A good infantry unit cross-trains its soldiers on its many weapon types so that everyone is proficient at firing a rifle, M249 machine gun, M203 grenade launcher, and other assigned systems. Commanders should similarly plan for having to operate with other services, coalition members, or agencies. Familiarization is the minimum standard; cooperative training (before entering the area of operations if feasible) is much preferred. Such training should include everyone from the lowest-ranking soldier to commanders and their staffs.

Be aware that urban densities compress the operational area and can result in more incidents of fratricide.

Densities make unusual demands on units. Artillery units will at times split batteries into sections in order to compensate for difficult angles of fire and dead space found when buildings are present. This decentralization will require greater proficiency by officers and non-commissioned officers (NCOs) who would otherwise not be operating independently. And as maneuver units are similarly likely to operate in smaller echelons (e.g., greater physical separation between squads), their personnel must be able to handle tasks generally left to more senior individuals. Calling for fire, land navigation, and negotiation skills are but three examples.

The increased risks of fratricide should these leaders be inadequately trained are readily apparent. The fratricide need not be limited to those on the receiving end of outgoing rounds. Concussion from artillery, tank, and other large ordnance can wound or kill. Setting up guns in an enclosed area such as a walled parking lot can cause internal injuries that become apparent only after the fatal damage is done. Likewise, proper selection of munitions will be key. Tank main gun concussion can injure. So can the sabots discarded when anti-armor or multipurpose anti-tank (MPAT) rounds are fired if unprotected personnel are too close to the front of the vehicle. It should be noted that M2 Bradley main guns sometimes also fire sabot ammunition.

Densities affect even the lowest echelons. In an open area it is frequently possible for a single crewmember to provide adequate security for his vehicle while others rest. But in a built-up area, the number of nearby buildings and consequent potential firing positions or approach routes means that even two or three crew members may not be enough to meet the demands of such a task. Assigning such vehicles to duties that demand tasks in addition to security alone, e.g., manning a checkpoint, places further burden on small crews. Commanders need to consider a more frequent rotation of personnel or unusual task organizations to meet the demands of such contingencies. A resultant reorganization might well influence equipment as well as personnel assignments. The range of weapons available to a tank crew is impressive (from a 120mm main gun to a 9mm pistol), but those men lack the individual or smaller crew-served weapons (e.g., M4 carbines) needed to meet the varied demands of establishing a roadblock or performing other checkpoint-related tasks.[43] All of these factors can increase stress.

Cities pose their own safety hazards even in the absence of an enemy. A soldier in Mogadishu was killed when he accidentally activated the ejection seat in an old Somali air force MiG aircraft at the airport. Three others were killed by sharks while swimming in the waters near the city. One was a soldier in Colonel Gore's command who had disobeyed the commander's orders to "not even put a toe in

---

[43] William A. Kendrick, "Peacekeeping Operations in Somalia," *Infantry*, May–June 1995, p. 33.

the water" after previous incidents. Proximity to garbage and human waste likewise increases the risk of disease. Personal hygiene will be critical to maintaining operational strength and morale. The number of nonbattle risks are likely to be greater than leaders can monitor. Colonel Gore recommends routine discussions with medical personnel to determine causes of nonbattle loss so that remedies can be identified.[44]

Get the ROE right as quickly as possible.

It is at the tactical level that the implications of ROE are most personally felt. It is the infantryman who has to expose himself to additional danger if he is proscribed from tossing a fragmentation grenade through the door before entry. (The danger is magnified if his leadership failed to requisition sufficient flash-bang grenades to use as distracters in such cases.) Lives, morale, and chain of command legitimacy are on the line when leaders sit down to determine rules of engagement.

The doctrinal definition is another that technically limits its application to situations involving combat:

> **Rules of Engagement**—Directives issued by competent military authority that delineate the circumstances and limitations under which United States forces *will initiate and/or continue combat engagement with other forces encountered.*[45]

Any guidance on interactions with noncombatants or with potential combatants in a noncombat situation does not comprise ROE if one adheres to this definition. Such material can certainly be put in an operations order's coordinating instructions or an appendix, but commanders might find it useful to expand the ROE definition somewhat when operating in built-up areas. First, there is unquestionably a need to make it clear to soldiers when they are authorized to put civilians at risk (e.g., when noncombatants are being used as

---

[44] Gore interview.

[45] Joint Publication 1-02, p. 461 (emphasis added).

shields by an enemy engaging friendly forces). While it is technically the enemy being engaged, there is no doubt that the ROE should address the likelihood that friendly-force fire will put civilians in mortal danger. Second, it might make sense to include noncombat related guidance in ROE to cover "gray areas" of engagement, e.g., when the threat or actual use of lethal force might be necessary for force protection or other security reasons during a riot or demonstration. Third, commanders may find the use of ROE in other than the doctrinal sense to be valuable during operations that do not involve combat. For example, the definition precludes the use of ROE for nonlethal engagements when combat is not an element. The discussion that follows includes these and other extradoctrinal cases.

Flexibility and insight are crucial to proper ROE design. The myriad challenges inherent in any urban undertaking mean that it is impossible to cover all operational contingencies during war games or rehearsals. ROE creators have to provide guidance for nonlethal engagements in addition to those involving lethal force. These will obviously include instances involving the use of nonlethal systems or munitions (although it should be recognized that many so-called nonlethal weapons may on occasion be lethal to some members of the population), but they also include other interactions such as employing threats of force, psychological operations, demonstrations of force, degradation or destruction of equipment, and other approaches with possible utility. Complete prohibition of the use of artillery support, for example, might be unproductive if a commander can instead use those system capabilities in negotiation. An example might be allowing the nonlethal firing of one or more artillery rounds into a vacant area to back up a negotiating point with the objective of saving lives and time that would otherwise be consumed in follow-on combat operations. Other nonstandard uses of force could include employing the heat from Abrams tank exhaust to influence crowd behavior. Approaching crowds with mine plows, pointing weapons at individuals, and performing low-level aircraft overflights have all been used for their intimidation effect in the past.[46] Colonel Gore's avia-tors found that "having the 20mm gun in flex mode was very effec-tive. The Somalis called the Cobras 'the bird that throws stones.' If you started moving the gun, they'd start running if they'd ever seen it shoot before."[47] It is also widely understood that nonlethal use should generally include contingent readiness to apply lethal force. ROE should encompass such circumstances, many of which involve other than "combat engagement with other forces."

Flexibility when contemplating rules of engagement includes de-fining "engagement" in its full spectrum of possibilities. During sup-port and stability operations, concerns will frequently be more tuned to local sensitivities and longer-term relations than to life-and-death decisions. Commanders need to ensure that the guidance their sol-diers or marines receive is no less practical than in more threatening situations. Lieutenant William Kendrick, writing on his security re-sponsibilities in Mogadishu, recalled that his unit

> could not remove brush because of possible violations of Somali land rights. We had to send requests for land clearance to the joint task force, just as we did for indirect fire, and these requests were normally disapproved. For this reason, our fields of fire of-ten extended no more than 50 meters, and the possibility of a lone gunman crawling up through the brush concerned us greatly. At Checkpoint 31, our fields of fire were no more than 100 meters wide, and we received sniper fire from little more than that distance on several occasions.[48]

It is not enough simply to provide well-considered ROE to a unit. Personnel should be challenged by situations that fall into "gray areas" during training so that they are better able to deal with tough decisions when they confront them during actual operations. Retired Brigadier General Gideon Avidor suggests that individuals should use an ROE checklist in which they consider whether the situation

---

[46] Kendrick, "Peacekeeping Operations in Somalia," p. 33.

[47] Gore interview.

[48] Kendrick, "Peacekeeping Operations in Somalia," p. 34.

- involves self-defense;
- provides for the use of alternatives other than lethal force to defend oneself or the unit;
- could preclude mission accomplishment or have other immediate and highly significant immediate consequences;
- could affect higher-level objectives or long-term success, e.g., local or international public opinion.

Leaders would of course adapt the specifics of checklist content and training exercises depending on the demands of a mission and its environment.[49]

Other engagement-related concerns include definitions of "danger close"; choice of munitions, weapons, or systems in various situations; and limits on vehicle movement.[50]

There is call for research on what constitutes danger close in built-up areas. The presence of buildings between a target and friendly forces, the condition of those structures, the material they are built of, and other factors are likely to mitigate a given munitions definition of danger close (and thus the rules of engagement for its use). ROE need to establish standards based on good judgment by those most familiar with the weapon systems in question in the absence of such research.

Other system capabilities and weapon characteristics will also influence which means of engagement are best suited to given situations. Arguably the Cobra helicopter is better suited to some urban fighting than is the Apache. The warhead and flight-trajectory characteristics of the TOW versus the Hellfire missile mean that calling on TOW-equipped Cobras could at times mitigate the extent of collateral damage. Similar choices will exist when considering whether to employ certain fixed-wing aircraft, artillery, mortar, or other systems.

---

[49] Provided to authors in General Avidor's review comments.

[50] Danger close: In close air support, artillery, mortar, and naval gunfire support fires, it is the term included in the method of engagement segment of a call for fire which indicates that friendly forces are within close proximity of the target. The close proximity distance is determined by the weapon and munitions fired. See Joint Publication 1-02, p. 140.

The advantages and disadvantages of each given the types of urban conditions a commander expects to confront should be identified before operations begin. Such analysis then allows responsible staff and line leaders to develop ROE guidance on what to use under which conditions.

See the forest *and* selected trees.

Vision and *coup d'oeil* during tactical-level urban operations in considerable part come down to knowing how much to centralize or decentralize in given situations. While more a matter of control, command and leadership influence these choices. Physical conditions will play a part. The degree of compartmentalization, proximity of other friendly forces, and vertical displacement between units are examples of factors that will facilitate or hinder centralization. Personality and expertise will directly influence whether an individual is given greater or lesser autonomy. Two individuals holding the same type of position might well be granted different amounts of leeway depending on their commander's confidence in each. As already noted, the task in question and the availability of given resources will likewise affect the desirable degree of centralization; some low-density capabilities might be centralized in an effort to make them more responsive to other, widely distributed assets.

A commander's position will directly influence his perspective on a battle. Flying overhead will give him a macro perspective virtually impossible to obtain from a position on the streets and in the alleys below . . . unless most activity is taking place within buildings. Remaining at a tactical operations center (TOC) could provide a happy medium between obtaining information on the "big picture" and understanding conditions on the ground. However, communications may be intermittent, making it difficult to command at all. A commander might therefore choose to move forward with a small ad hoc TOC, either mounted or dismounted, or simply settle for moving forward himself with only a radio operator. The benefits of the last option include close contact with actual operational conditions, frequent opportunities to interact with subordinates, and a chance to thereby influence morale and monitor levels of exhaustion. On the downside, communications with other subordinates, the TOC, and higher headquarters could suffer interruptions. The commander's risks of becoming enmeshed in local activities or getting killed or wounded are higher. The essence of the decision on where to be is no different in an urban operation than in any other. The proper decision will depend on the situation. However, there is an increased likelihood of being out of touch, lost, or unable to move to a desired location when the environment is an urban one. The commander will inevitably be challenged to maintain an effective perspective of both the forest and the trees. A well articulated and clearly communicated intent combined with subordinates trained for decentralized operations allow a commander to provide a sense of his *coup d'oeil* and vision to subordinate leaders.

Control During Urban Operations

Having considered the command and leadership element of battle command, the second component to receive attention is control. FM 6-0 proposes the following as a definition for control:

> The regulation of forces and other battlefield operating systems (BOS) to accomplish the mission in accordance with the commander's intent. It includes collecting, processing, displaying, storing, and disseminating relevant information for creating the common operational picture and using information during the operations process.[51]

A primary difference between command and control is that an individual has a lot of help with the latter. Only a commander commands; ultimately the key decisions are his and much rides on his expertise, judgment, and composure at critical times during an operation. The multiplicity of functions inherent in regulating and otherwise providing control are shared between a commander, his

---

[51] Field Manual 6-0, p. Glossary-3.

subordinate leaders, his staff, and every disciplined soldier or marine assigned to his organization.

The following categories are covered in this discussion.

Control During Urban Operations

Look deeper in time and beyond military considerations during the backward planning process.	
Consider second- and higher-order effects during planning and war gaming.	
Doctrine asks lower-echelon leaders to look two levels up. Higher-echelon commanders need to consider the limits and perspectives of same nation and other subordinate headquarters and units. Commanders at every echelon need to be conscious of the situation as it impacts those at higher, lower, adjacent, joint, multinational, and interagency levels.	✔
Account for the language, cultural, procedural, and other differences that will impede the tempo and level of understanding when dealing with some coalition member units and other agencies.	✔
Be aware that urban densities compress the operational area and can result in more incidents of fratricide.	✔
Get the ROE right as quickly as possible.	✔
See the forest *and* selected trees.	✔

Doctrine asks lower-echelon leaders to look two levels up. Higher-echelon commanders need to consider the limits and perspectives of same nation (and other) subordinate headquarters and units.

As just noted, control is "the regulation of forces and other battlefield operating systems (BOS) to accomplish the mission *in accordance with the commander's intent.*" The commander's intent exists in part because commanders know they cannot oversee and regulate everything themselves. Nor can they provide guidance or write orders that cover every possible contingency that might arise during a mission. The intent is one mechanism of control. Another is the extent to which a commander allows a subordinate freedom of action in working within that intent: the level of centralization or decentralization of control. Joint Publication 3-06, *Doctrine for Joint Urban Operations*, described the relationship between these concepts:

In urban areas, ground operations tend to become decentralized. It is therefore highly important that C2 be flexible, adaptive, and decentralized as well. Essential to decentralized C2 is the thorough knowledge and understanding of the commander's intent at every level of command. To further enhance decentralized C2, commanders at all levels should issue mission-type orders and use implicit communications wherever possible.[52]

Previous discussion covered the command factors that influence the degree of centralization a commander chooses to require. Many control-related elements will also influence the extent to which a leader or organization is allowed free rein. The greater density of friendly and enemy forces, together with the difficulties in obtaining and communicating ISR information, increases the risk of fratricide. Control measures that specify areas (volumes) in which a unit can move and fire are critical to not inadvertently killing or wounding a soldier in an adjacent unit.[53] The high density of demands on units means that they may be in neighboring buildings or even on different floors or in different hallways of the same building. Inadequate control measures mean that a soldier might fire through a wall or ceiling into another unit's area of operation. Traditionally the careful planning necessary, which involves very explicit control measures and related guidance, is called centralized planning. Its objective is to articulate with great clarity and thoroughness the bounds of allowable action such that a leader then has considerable freedom of action as long as he operates within those constraints. In short, urban operations demand centralized planning and decentralized execution of those plans.

Urban operations tend to require decentralization of maneuver elements because of the inability to see more than a limited part of

---

[52] Joint Publication 3-06, *Doctrine for Joint Urban Operations*, Washington, D.C.: Joint Chiefs of Staff, September 16, 2002, p. III-4.

[53] Options for control range from command arrangements that establish explicit engagement zones for each unit to more dynamic arrangements that require some coordination between the units. In practice, flexibility between the two options is required, depending on available communications and friendly force information.

the area of operation, communicate consistently, or maintain satisfactory situational awareness in so complex an environment. Colonel Johnny Brooks, who as a lieutenant colonel commanded a task force during Operation Just Cause in Panama, concurs. He found that during his 1989 urban combat operations he could not "see anything to affect anything. There has to be a great trust there. Whether you are a centralized commander or decentralized commander makes no difference. In urban operations everyone is a decentralized commander."[54] Vasili Chuikov wrote that his Soviet commanders similarly found themselves with less ability to control their forces during fighting in World War II Stalingrad than had been the case in more open terrain prior to that battle.[55]

Brooks goes on to suggest a way of in part overcoming the aforementioned difficulty in managing low-density assets such as medics or engineers. The authors previously noted that a commander might be compelled to hold these assets back in a central location the better to dispatch them to the location most needed when they are in demand. Brooks found that he simply did not have enough in the way of support assets to evacuate casualties, bring supplies forward, and accomplish other tasks. Therefore, many tasks generally left to specialists became common responsibilities. He concludes that "everybody has to be a jack of all trades."[56] The argument for providing squad members with additional skills such as those possessed by Combat Lifesavers is obvious. Brooks's experiences are similar to those of commanders fighting in urban areas many years earlier.

Decentralization puts additional burdens on commanders. They cannot conduct decentralized operations if they have not previously trained their subordinates for the responsibilities that decentralization imposes on them. Higher-level commanders do not cede that responsibility; ultimately the success or failure is theirs. But those more

---

[54] Brooks interview.

[55] The authors thank LTC Mike Chura for bringing the observation on Vasili Chuikov to their attention.

[56] Brooks interview.

junior leaders will have to manage a greater variety and number of tasks than might otherwise be the case. They will also have to exercise judgment in evaluating situations, and do so at a level that can push the limits of their expertise. Here, too, training and pre-operation leadership can make a considerable difference. Sometimes the right decision can be the counterintuitive one. Taking an example from other than military experience, the courage of off-duty police and fire personnel and those from other jurisdictions who rushed to assist rescue operations at the World Trade Center on September 11, 2001 are justifiably admired. However, from an objective perspective their decision to go to the disaster site is reason for concern. A subsequent evaluation of the events that day included the conclusion that "the city's intricate network of safety coverage showed signs of unraveling that morning because of the headlong rush to Lower Manhattan . . . . Too many came without being told they were needed."[57] Former New York City Fire Commissioner Thomas Von Essen summed up the concern: "There's a lack of control that's dangerous on an everyday basis . . . . Courage is not enough . . . . The fact that the guys are so dedicated comes back to hurt them down the line."[58] Military training needs to prepare leaders to appropriately handle the unexpected. Given a massive explosion several blocks away, do they react to assist (given a lack of communications that keeps them from contacting their leaders)? The correct answer will depend on the situation, mission, and other factors. Response to this, or any other unexpected event not explicitly covered in orders or rehearsals, could be a case of wisely "moving to the sound of the guns." On the other hand, the explosion might be an enemy attempt at a diversion, meaning that massing in that area leaves another area unsecured or sets the preconditions for a successful chemical strike.

Urban complexity makes extraordinary demands on every part of an organization: the commander, his staff, subordinate leaders,

---

[57] Jim Dwyer et al., "9/11 Exposed Deadly Flaws in Rescue Plan," *The New York Times*, July 7, 2002. Online at http://www.nytimes.com/2002/07/07/nyreg.../07emer.html, accessed April 22, 2003.

[58] Ibid.

supporting units, and the individual soldier. The potential for a tempo involving an extremely large number of events per unit time requires that every part know its responsibilities and that it has been trained to handle them. Lee Gore designated that his staff would assume full control of some critical events. They had the responsibility to properly respond to a downed aircraft, for example.[59] Colonel Gore realized that he would have to continue commanding those aircraft still flying and thus could not abandon them to oversee recovery operations. Regardless of the type of unit, commanders need to develop contingency plans, rehearse them, and train their personnel so that they respond properly when the tempo of operations becomes so high that every organizational component is heavily tasked.

It is interesting that an author describing operations over St. George's, the capital of Grenada, wrote that "the same lessons that TF 160 had learned earlier had been drummed home again in the afternoon: unsupported helicopters over St. George's invited disaster."[60] This was a full decade before the loss of Black Hawk helicopters over Mogadishu. Repeated losses of rotary-wing aircraft over built-up areas means that most leaders at any echelon understand the risks they take when committing helicopters to support urban combat. Less well understood is the difficulty of conducting airspace control in the environment. Increasing use of UAVs means that the task will become harder yet. Colonel Gore recalled that his single greatest problem with airspace control over Mogadishu was due primarily to a medical evacuation (MEDEVAC) unit's lack of experience and cooperation. While TF 160, 10th Mountain Division, and 101st Air Assault aviation personnel all adhered to control procedures, the medical aviators caused considerable problems by flying through other units' gun lines and generally either disregarding or acting in ignorance of other ongoing aviation activities. The density of military actions in the city were such that what might have passed as annoyances in more open terrain became potentially very dangerous episodes in

---

[59] Gore interview.

[60] Mark Adkin, *Urgent Fury: The Battle for Grenada*, London: Leo Cooper, 1989, p. 245.

Somalia. Colonel Gore recommended that medical evacuation aircraft in the future be subordinate to the local aviation brigade or other aviation commander rather than the medical commander.[61]

It is notable that while problems with other units did not reach the level experienced with MEDEVAC personnel, there was less coordination between special operations and regular force aviators than Colonel Gore thought healthy. Panama and Somalia are but two examples of such forces having to operate in closer proximity. Greater cooperation is called for. Control measures in many cases need not impinge on operation security. Assigning air corridors and elevations to given organizations can aid in reducing coordination traffic while also speeding modifications to standing control procedures.

Urban terrain and its more malevolent occupants will further contrive to make aviators' lives arduous. The "brown out" conditions caused by the effects of rotor wash on Mogadishu's dusty streets exemplify one such challenge. Winds tend to swirl in urban environments, meaning that dust and smoke generated when rounds strike a target can quickly obscure the surrounding area. This can make providing further fire support difficult if not impossible until the obstacle to sight clears. The sun can likewise pose problems. Colonel Gore noted that in Somalia "the sun was a real problem." Flying late in the afternoon or early in the morning when the sun was near the horizon, "we couldn't see anything." The night brought its own problems. Lights from the city reflected off the clouds to silhouette helicopters against a background that made them easy to spot from below. Residents attempting to interfere with coalition operations flew kites and strung wire between tall buildings in efforts to down U.S. helicopters.[62]

FM 3-06.1, *Aviation Urban Operations,* notes that "navigation over urban terrain can be more difficult than over natural terrain due to an over-abundance of cues . . . . The high density of structures, variety of geographical references, and high light levels can create

---

[61] Gore interview.

[62] Material in this paragraph is taken from the Gore interview.

'visual saturation.'"[63] The manual goes on to suggest that the density of aircraft over a built-up area might justify establishing a Restricted Operations Zone (ROZ) or high-density airspace control zone (HIDACZ) to allow for the management of the several types of aircraft likely to be operating simultaneously.[64] The designation of routes should capitalize on easily recognizable terrain features, while maintaining the required flexibility. Tall buildings, cemeteries, parks, stadiums, and other prominent features are good for day navigation. Lights can make nighttime flying especially difficult. Features such as parks and cemeteries (with their absence of light) are therefore effective as landmarks.[65]

As previously noted, urban operations need not be limited to actions in built-up areas. Interdiction or other deep operations could involve strikes tens or even hundreds of kilometers distant from the metropolitan area itself. (On the other hand, "deep" operations within an urban area might be only tens of blocks away from friendly forces.) Actions taken to isolate a town or city will most likely have to be coordinated with those within the confines of the urban entity. Internal and external activities will compete for resources. Effective control will require leaders to find the appropriate balance between in-city operations (probably receiving the bulk of media, and perhaps therefore higher headquarters', attention) and those in more open terrain.

While challenging, control of air operations rarely achieves the level of difficulty experienced by those on the ground. Reverberation of noise off hard surfaces; smoke, walls, and other barriers to sight and radio waves; high personnel casualty rates; and a lack of readily identifiable terrain features conspire to defeat a commander's efforts to maintain control. Once lost, that control is difficult to restore. Complicated plans and drills will founder, especially if a leader be-

---

[63] Field Manual 3-06.1, *Aviation Urban Operations: Multiservice Procedures for Aviation Urban Operations*, Fort Monroe, VA: U.S. Army Training and Doctrine Command, April 2001, p. III-9.

[64] Ibid., p. III-4.

[65] Ibid., pp. III-7 and III-9.

comes a casualty. Simplicity helps soldiers maintain or regain their bearings under pressure.[66] The same control measures that work elsewhere will assist in maintaining control during urban undertakings. More phase lines, checkpoints, contact points, clearly delineated boundaries, and casualty collection points will probably be designated in an urban area of operations than in more open terrain. Assigning code numbers, letters, or names to sectors of the built-up area and specific features (most notably buildings) will help to reduce misunderstandings about locations and where fire support is required. (Marines in Iraq during the 2003 Operation Iraqi Freedom divided built-up areas into colored zones with numbered sections for targeting and coordination.)[67] At the lowest levels, units need to designate and train using multiple means of communicating, to include voice, hand signals, smoke, lasers, radio, and others. Most important, soldiers must always be ready to improvise. A forward air controller with the 1st/75th Rangers used reflections from a mirror to designate a building housing an enemy recoilless rifle during fighting in Grenada. Two Cobra helicopter pilots previously unable to distinguish where their support was called for then destroyed the target.[68]

Historically, extended urban operations have led to nontraditional task organizations. The assignment of individual vehicles to support infantry squads or platoons was mentioned early in this report. Marines in 1968 Hue paired their highly survivable M60 tanks with quick but virtually unprotected Ontos 90mm gun carriers to provide infantry with needed fire support. General Vasili Chuikov writes that storm groups became the norm during 1942–43 fighting in Stalingrad. Storm groups consisted of the following:

- Assault groups consisting of six to eight men each whose duty was to break into buildings "and wage battle independently inside it."

---

[66] Army Field Manual Volume 2, "Operations in Specific Environments," Part 5, 4-24, pp. 48–49, *Urban Operations*, British Army, 1999.

[67] Russell Rafferty, email to Russell W. Glenn, "OIF Marine Recap," June 6, 2003.

[68] Adkin, *Urgent Fury: The Battle for Grenada*, p. 216.

- Reinforcement groups that entered the buildings as soon as the assault groups made successful entries. They broke into the same buildings via different entry points, thereafter establishing firing positions to prevent the reinforcement of enemy units fighting the assault groups. Whereas the assault group was quite lightly equipped and manned solely with infantry, reinforcement groups had heavy machine guns, anti-tank rifles, and explosives.

- Reserve groups acted to reinforce assault groups or interdict outside attacks on the buildings that assault and reinforcement groups had entered. As necessary, they could be the basis for the formation of additional assault groups.[69]

During the three weeks of intensive fighting in Hue, U.S. marines retained their traditional organizations with the exception of the vehicular support. Organizations will be a function of the threat, units available, mission, terrain, and other factors. As is the case with coalition forces, task organizing early to allow planning, rehearsing, and establishment of internal standing operating procedures (SOPs) is critical.

Account for the language, cultural, procedural, and other differences that will impede the tempo and level of understanding when dealing with some coalition member units and other agencies.

Working with other service, multinational, or interagency representatives should spur an even greater focus on following proven planning and order procedures than is the case within a commander's own unit. The value of clearly articulating orders, both verbally and graphically, and rehearsing plans is magnified when some parts of a team are unfamiliar with traditional service approaches. It may well be insufficient to simply adjust the 1/3–2/3 rule to allow multinational partners to gain more preparation time. Assignment of liaison personnel qualified to assist in orders development and the conduct of rehearsals could pay major dividends during execution. Liaison

---

[69] Vasili I. Chuikov, *The Battle for Stalingrad,* New York: Holt, Rinehart, and Winston, 1964, p. 294.

personnel are too often viewed simply as messengers with compatible radio communications. They will diplomatically have to play a much more intrusive role when the level of a fellow coalition member's headquarters is not up to the professional standards demanded by operational effectiveness.

It may also be necessary to adapt control procedures to facilitate interactions with either coalition partners or other agencies. If coalition partners have fewer communications and ISR assets, tighter controls may be needed near areas where they are operating. Liaison with local officials is simplified if they have a single point of contact, which can be facilitated by taking not only military needs into account when determining control zones, but also existing areas of responsibility for and interactions between local agencies including councils, religious organizations, and police and fire departments.[70]

Such relationships are further complicated by sometimes overly conservative classification procedures. Overhead imagery will frequently be the only way that units can acquire tools for navigation and coordination that meet their requirements for scale, level of detail, and responsiveness. Even U.S. units at times still have problems obtaining such imagery due to classification issues. Multinational units suffer even greater restraints. Given the plethora of overhead imagery sources now available (even on the open market), reconsideration of classification guidelines is long overdue. One approach would be to declassify low-resolution or pixilated versions of otherwise classified images. Although insufficient for intelligence purposes, such images should be good enough for coordination and navigation.[71]

Be aware that urban densities compress the operational area and can result in more incidents of fratricide.

---

[70] Allison interview and John P. Miller interview with Russell W. Glenn, Gina Kingston, Les Dishman, and Steve Hartman, Hollywood, California, May 15, 2003.

[71] This idea is based on comments by Col Jay Bruder. Jay Bruder and J. D. Wilson, interview with Gina Kingston, Quantico, Virginia, May 27, 2003.

The difficulties with maps, imagery, and accuracy in navigating or calling for fires in urban areas are as yet too little appreciated. The use of six-digit grid coordinates is the accepted norm in many units. Such accuracy designates a location to within 100 meters, normally sufficient for designating information in open terrain. "I am in the woods located at AB 123456" will generally get a subordinate to his senior's headquarters. Adjusting artillery fire from coordinates within 100 meters of a target is straightforward. One-hundred-meter visibility from a city street may be a luxury (other than along the axis of that street). Providing an ambulance crew with 100-meter accuracy to guide their recovering wounded could put them on the wrong side of a city block or river with no idea in which direction the soldier in need might be. GPS can help. In many instances it will. In others, especially from positions located within structures (as hospitals, headquarters, and other vital military nodes are wont to be), walls or other barriers may block GPS signals.

These difficulties further argue for the provision of unclassified detailed imagery to the lowest levels, in appropriate cases even to members of private voluntary organizations (PVOs) or NGOs. Overlaying the images with a uniform grid and location code, one shared by all users, would facilitate more effective and sufficient support of all types while reducing the chances of fratricide or inadvertent entry into known high-threat areas.

Get the ROE right as quickly as possible.

Interactions with civilian governmental personnel will be fairly straightforward during most urban combat operations. Military commanders will provide guidance to indigenous personnel to best ensure their safety and that of friendly-force personnel. Relationships will become more complicated as fighting ends or in instances where military personnel are supporting domestic civilian government agencies. Legal advice will be crucial to a commander's understanding his responsibilities and the limits to his authority during such contingencies.

One such challenge, and a notably difficult one for military leaders, is riot or demonstration control. Such events can involve hundreds or thousands of indigenous personnel. They can be staged by enemies of the friendly force who want to discredit coalition objectives or used as a cover for other activities. In many cases they include some organizers/instigators who may or may not be armed. Other members of the crowd can be active supporters of the instigators, sympathizers, paid demonstrators, or others that include innocent passers-by inadvertently caught up in the activity. Women and children are frequently part of the crowd and can be employed as witting or unwitting shields for armed personnel or instigators.

It is unfortunate, but to date most of the military investment in nonlethal capabilities has gone to individual or point systems (e.g., rubber bullets) that have limited utility in many demonstration and riot scenarios. Systems under development, to include microwave and directed energy capabilities, might offer relief in this regard. Martin N. Stanton suggests in his "Riot Control for the 1990s" that it is a good rule of thumb to focus on eliminating lethal threats in a crowd before dealing with the remainder, even in cases where the lethal threat is very small in size as compared to the crowd at large.[72]

Organizing to meet riot contingencies demands task organizing in a manner not dramatically different from Chuikov's observations on urban fighting in World War II Stalingrad. One author recommends using four components, of which only the last differs significantly from those proposed by Chuikov:

1. **Riot control.** Those on the ground in close proximity to the rioters or demonstrators, likely to be in formation.

2. **Overwatch.** Personnel maintaining oversight of the riot control element with the particular responsibility to protect its personnel from lethal threats.

3. **Reserve.** Personnel prepared to reinforce or otherwise complement the riot control component as necessary to contain, direct, or otherwise influence the crowd.

---

[72] Martin N. Stanton, "Riot Control for the 1990s," *Infantry,* January–February 1996, pp. 26–27.

4. **Special purpose.** Organizations with a specialized specific function such as application of a particular technology or the use of dogs.[73]

Dealing with demonstrations or riots demands no less in the way of training or combined arms synchronization than other operations. APCs, infantry fighting vehicles, and tanks are excellent for intimidation, transporting personnel, or other uses during such contingencies. The light armored vehicle (LAV) was repeatedly cited for its effectiveness in this regard by Australian leaders who commanded in East Timor. Soldier training should include planning for, employment of, and target practice with nontraditional systems (e.g., tear gas or other nonlethal capabilities such as pepper spray).[74] Leaders and subordinates should also practice negotiation techniques, rapid barrier erection, techniques for redirecting crowds, and techniques for identifying crowd manipulators.

Such public control actions can be part of a larger event involving many loosely or uncoordinated activities over a large area, some of which may be peaceful while others involve the use or threat of lethal force. During the 1992 Los Angeles riots, California Army National Guard leaders sent two companies 40 miles northeast of the city to assist in containing a prison riot.[75] These contingencies may also require supplementary communications capabilities to orchestrate ongoing activities and provide connectivity with indigenous civilian public service agencies.[76]

Riot control is not the only role in which military commanders face nontraditional threats requiring adaptive tactics. The ability to deal with suicide bombers and other terrorist tactics during peace-enforcement or combat operations is especially challenging in an urban environment due to the presence of noncombatants. ROE will

---

[73] Ibid., p. 27.

[74] Ibid., p. 28.

[75] William V. Wenger, "The Los Angeles Riots: A Battalion Commander's Perspective," *Infantry*, January–February 1994, p. 14.

[76] Ibid., p. 15.

have to be fairly restrictive. Leaders will therefore have to develop procedures and conduct training for effectively identifying and neutralizing such threats remotely from friendly forces and other prospective targets.

See the forest *and* selected trees.

The complexity of day-to-day actions during missions in cities can blind leaders to longer-term and broader responsibilities. Postcombat operations in Panama and Baghdad remind one that urban operations do not become any less complex when the fighting stops. What changes is the nature of the challenges. Just as the end state from which staff personnel should begin their backward planning needs to encompass more than military concerns, so should branches, sequels, and contingency plans likewise take this wider and deeper-in-time perspective.[77] Rarely will that end state not include a civil component at the higher tactical and operational levels. The desire to preserve noncombatant life and infrastructure will therefore significantly affect combat planning.

Flexibility in plans and control will be critical to success during postcombat (or noncombat) operations no less than those involving fighting. The demands for agile forces and synchronization will be just as great. Lee Gore recalled how the routine could quickly become the extraordinary during his time in Mogadishu:

> Any operation could become a major operation in a moment. You send a bulldozer to move a roadblock and all of a sudden they'd have thousands of people come out of the woodwork. Any time ground forces went out, I had someone in the air and had everyone else loaded for bear and ready. In the city you couldn't control the battlefield like you could a linear battlefield. Little engagements turned into major firefights all the time.[78]

Complexity and high tempo can cause leaders and staffs to become too focused on immediate issues. "Pushing away from the ta-

---

[77] Joint Publication 3-06, p. III-6.

[78] Gore interview.

ble" to deliberately view the bigger picture should be a conscious effort that is regularly exercised.

ISR During Urban Operations

Intelligence, surveillance, and reconnaissance considerations related to urban operations have in considerable part been covered in previous RAND research and are therefore addressed relatively briefly here.[79] As in the case of control just completed, the authors analyze the challenges at both the tactical and operational levels.

The following categories are covered in this discussion.

ISR During Urban Operations

Look deeper in time and beyond military considerations during the backward planning process.	
Consider second- and higher-order effects during planning and war gaming.	
Doctrine asks lower-echelon leaders to look two levels up. Higher-echelon commanders need to consider the limits and perspectives of same nation and other subordinate headquarters and units. Commanders at every echelon need to be conscious of the situation as it impacts those at higher, lower, adjacent, joint, multinational, and interagency levels.	
Account for the language, cultural, procedural, and other differences that will impede the tempo and level of understanding when dealing with some coalition member units and other agencies.	✔
Be aware that urban densities compress the operational area and can result in more incidents of fratricide.	
Get the ROE right as quickly as possible.	
See the forest *and* selected trees.	✔

---

[79] See Russell W. Glenn et al., *Honing the Keys to the City: Refining the United States Marine Corps Reconnaissance Force for Urban Ground Operations*, Santa Monica, CA: RAND Corporation, MR-1628-USMC, 2003.

Account for the language, cultural, procedural, and other differences that will impede the tempo and level of understanding when dealing with some coalition member units and other agencies.

Intelligence procedures are typically problematic when dealing with members of foreign nations—including coalition members, local government authorities, and other agencies. In many cases, each coalition member and agency will each have its own intelligence collection activities, in line with its own agendas.[80] Information releasability between coalition participants varies. Much intelligence information is initially classified NOFORN and can only be released to coalition partners after reclassification.[81] This not only causes delays in operational tempo but can also complicate international relationships and is a potential source of confusion about what information can be discussed with various parties.[82]

Sharing of intelligence with civilian organizations is in many situations critical but even more problematic. Local authorities, PVOs, and NGOs are often in a better position to collect certain types of information than military forces. There are challenges for both parties wishing to share information. The military is unwilling to share information because of security concerns; PVOs and NGOs may be unwilling to share information because it can adversely affect their reputation for being unbiased and independent.

Even when information is transferred, it can be difficult to integrate with organic processing systems. For example, U.S. armed services use geographic data models that are at times based on standards different from those used by American civilian agencies.[83] The problem is more fundamental. Even the various U.S. armed forces persist

---

[80] Allison, interview with Kingston, June 6, 2003.

[81] Ibid.

[82] A discussion of the implications of not being able (or not choosing) to share intelligence with fellow coalition members appears in Russell W. Glenn et al., *Getting the Musicians of Mars on the Same Sheet of Music: Army Joint, Multinational, and Interagency C4ISR Interoperability*, Santa Monica, CA: RAND Corporation, DB-288-A, 2000, Unclassified/For Official Use Only. This document is not available to the general public.

[83] Ridenour and Ware interview.

in acquiring and employing intelligence systems incompatible with other armed forces despite joint command directives to do otherwise. The problems are magnified when the United States considers working with coalition partners, local domestic agencies, and other interested parties.

The situation is further complicated by the presence of the media, which is often able to broadcast information faster than the military.[84] Military mechanisms are slower for a variety of reasons, including security concerns, intermediate processing (which means that information is assessed and filtered as it passes through an organization), and the desire to pass some information face-to-face for purposes of clarity or morale. For example, several news organizations reported the identities of U.S. prisoners of war captured during Operation Iraqi Freedom before their families had been informed by military authorities.

These issues are not specific to urban operations, but they have greater impact during urban contingencies due to the potential volume of intelligence; the increased interactions with PVOs, NGOs, and local authorities that are often required; and because of the increased accessibility of the media in built-up areas. Possible solutions include (1) increasing the emphasis on technical interoperability with other forces, services, and allies within the acquisition process, (2) developing procedures for transmitting unverified information, (3) improving multinational and interagency intelligence exchange agreements, and (4) developing control procedures to limit the requirements for the exchange of intelligence.

See the forest *and* selected trees.

Success during urban operations is, as elsewhere, dependent on effective intelligence. "Effective" implies accurate, timely, relevant, actionable, synchronized, and consistent. Unfortunately, the urban environment conspires to degrade accuracy, delay transmission or confirmation, mix the pertinent with the superfluous, interfere with translation to executable orders, impede links between intelligence

---

[84] Allison, interview with Kingston, June 6, 2003.

and maneuver units, and interrupt regular communication with providers. Overhead imagery, SIGINT, MASINT (measurements and signatures intelligence), and other means of collection can be spoofed, but the collection platforms are controlled, generally responsive, and the extent of their shortcomings known. Urban intelligence relies most heavily on the most inconsistent, unreliable, and least controllable of sources: human beings. As already noted, outright lies are commonplace, whether due to good intentions (wishing to please the recipient), self-interest (payment or protection), or a desire to deceive. A single source of intelligence can provide his product to several collection agencies, none of which synthesize their materials with other organizations until it is too late to determine that the many apparently independent and confirmatory inputs in fact originate from a single source. (Another problem is the product of many foreign intelligence organizations being players in influence games. British Army Brigadier Richard L. Clutterbuck recalled that during the Vietnam war "the repeated political and military coups have caused the intelligence organizations to devote more efforts to watching each other than to watching the Viet Cong.")[85] Validation of intelligence derived from collection means is frequently feasible when HUMINT is not involved. For example, the volume of communications from a particular building might indicate that it is a headquarters. Conducting UAV overflights that validate a heavy volume of traffic in and out of the structure would tend to confirm that suspicion. HUMINT can at times be confirmed via technological means, but often only another individual can lend credence to or discredit a given piece of information. Cultivation and control of agents and informers is time consuming and labor intensive. Protecting these sources can require extraordinary measures that introduce time delays into intelligence transmissions. Of course HUMINT can be employed to validate intelligence obtained by other means if time and the situation allow.[86]

---

[85] Richard L. Clutterbuck, *The Long, Long War: Counterinsurgency in Malaya and Vietnam*, New York: Praeger, 1966, p. 100.

[86] Luc Pigeon et al., *HUMINT Communication Information Systems for Complex Warfare*, Quebec: Defence R&D Canada Valcartier, undated, p. 2.

Correlating HUMINT can be difficult for additional reasons. A single individual may be known by a number of aliases and/or may act in different roles at different places and times.[87] But HUMINT also offers a depth of understanding that may be impossible to acquire via other means. Major General Rick Hiller, commander of UN forces in Bosnia-Herzegovina, recalled that his greatest need was to understand the interactions between various actors in a region, to go beyond simply what was happening to determine why it was happening and on whose authority.[88]

Even when confirmation by other means is not possible, however, HUMINT can still be invaluable, as U.S. forces learned after Tet 1968:

> There was a lack of SIGINT from [Viet Cong] units surrounding and infiltrating cities such as Hue because they did not generate heavy radio traffic. This resulted in dismissing other available information such as captured documents and prisoner interrogation reports that provided indications of impending attacks . . . .[89]

Greater reliance on resource-intensive HUMINT means that joint task force (JTF) and other headquarters will need more robust intelligence-processing capabilities—perhaps manned by those with different expertise than is called for in other environments. Urban densities mean that there are more sources of intelligence from which to draw. The greater density of actions per unit time mean that there will be a larger number of spot reports from friendly-force soldiers (presuming they are properly trained to input to the intelligence process) and more ambient activity to interfere with detection and

---

[87] Col Jay Bruder, in Jay Bruder and J. D. Wilson interview with Gina Kingston, Quantico, Virginia, May 27, 2003.

[88] In response to a question at the International Command and Control Symposium, Quebec City, September 2002. See also Slide 18 of his presentation, which is available at http://www.dod.ccrp.

[89] Maj. Bichson Bush, *Intelligence, Surveillance and Reconnaissance (ISR) Support to Urban Operations,* School of Advanced Military Studies, U.S. Army Command and General Staff College, Fort Leavenworth, KS, First Term AY 00–01.

screening of legitimate information. Furthermore, information provided by locals must at times undergo translation. Indigenous personnel will have their own names for locations and use slang that will have to be interpreted and, as necessary, translated into the map and grid references and code numbers used by the military.[90] The lower the echelon of the headquarters, the less well manned it will be to handle these challenges. A summary of a report by TRADOC noted that during a Joint Contingency Force (JCF) urban Advanced Warfighting Experiment (AWE) at Fort Polk,

> part of the information distribution problem was due to bottlenecks in the transmission pipeline . . . . Battalion operations center workstations . . . had less memory and processing speed. Personnel impacted information flow as well. At the AWE, there were "significantly" fewer personnel at the battalion level, particularly in the intelligence sections, to fuse the information, and they often had less experience than their counterparts at the brigade. Their workload was intense and sleep deprivation compounded the problem.[91]

An alternative to increasing the number (and seniority) of intelligence personnel at lower echelons is to put a greater burden on higher-level organizations for filtering and processing intelligence products before they are disseminated, thereby reducing the volume of input that subordinates have to deal with (though this alternative is less responsive to lower-echelon needs). Regardless of the method chosen to handle the problem, its solution is critical for many reasons, not the least of which is that a decision process deluged with information is more vulnerable to deception.[92]

It is apparent from the previous discussion that urban intelligence procedures, particularly those involving HUMINT collection,

---

[90] According to Col Jay Bruder, most SIGINT and HUMINT collected from locals is in terms of commercial references. Jay Bruder and J. D. Wilson, interview with Gina Kingston, Quantico, Virginia, May 27, 2003.

[91] "Experiment Results Show Room for Improvement in the Digital Army," *Inside The Army*, July 23, 2001, p. 5.

[92] Pigeon, *HUMINT Communication Information Systems for Complex Warfare*, p. 3.

may require nontraditional approaches. Operations in Somalia provide an example. U.S. leaders routinely met with clan and gang leaders in the early months of coalition operations in Mogadishu during the 1990s. Marine Lieutenant General Robert Johnston noted that "you may not like the characters you have to deal with but you are better able to uncover their motives and intentions if you keep a communications link open."[93] Ambassador Robert Oakley substantiated the value of these meetings, adding that they had considerable value beyond their serving as forums for intelligence collection. Speaking at an urban operations conference in March 2000, Oakley observed:

> The day Bob Johnston arrived, two days after the first marines landed, I was able to get Aideed and Ali Mahdi, the two principal commanders in Mogadishu, together for their first meeting since the civil war had started. Each of them brought 10 or 12 of their lieutenants.
>
> After about the fourth hour, Bob was complaining that he had more important things to do than to sit while these guys talked. I said "No, this is the most important thing you've got to do because they have to understand each other and they have to understand us. It's going to make it much less dangerous as we move ahead." At the end of it, the two leaders came up with a seven-point communiqué regarding a cease fire in Mogadishu. It covered removing roadblocks, getting the technicals and heavy weapons out of the way, not carrying arms on streets, and several other things that we, with a combination of persuasion and pressure, were actually able to get them to do within about 10 days. So by the tenth day the situation in Mogadishu was calm. You didn't have any shootings; you didn't find any arms being carried on the street; barricades were coming down.
>
> Somali leaders also wanted to set up a standing joint committee to continue such discussions. In part I think they liked the good food that we served them because nobody was getting very much to eat.

---

[93] Cooling, *Shaping the Battlespace*, p. 78.

But seriously, they understood the importance of talking. So every day for the rest of the time UNITAF was there, sometimes a dozen, sometimes 20 people, would meet at my compound to talk things over with each other and with us. I was often there; Bob Johnston was there; Tony Zinni was there. Sometimes we did it with somebody from my staff and one of the colonels, like Chip Gregson or Mike Hagey, but we were there to listen to them talk and to explain to them what we were doing so we didn't have any surprises. This didn't mean they always liked what we were doing. It didn't mean they agreed amongst themselves or with us, but there weren't many surprises.[94]

The increased reliance on HUMINT may otherwise cause deviations from standard procedure. It may be advisable, even essential, to seek the assistance of or even rely primarily on other than U.S. personnel when conducting intelligence and other information-related operations. Brigadier Clutterbuck, in writing of his experiences in putting down the Malay Rebellion during the 1960s, recalled that

> Government psychological-warfare material was written by Chinese, including a number of ex-Communists. The team was led by a forceful and imaginative Malayan Chinese, C. C. Too, who spent much time talking to surrendered guerrillas and studying captured documents. He was adept at forecasting their policies and reactions, and his psychological-warfare approach was based on the understanding gained from this constant contact with current Communist thinking. It took us some time to learn the obvious lesson that psychological warfare must be direct[ed] by a local man. It is amazing how many Europeans think they understand the Asian mind. The really able European, however, realized that their function was to provide good organization and enough supervision to insure against corruption and treachery, and to leave the intellectual contacts with Chinese guerrillas and

---

[94] Robert B. Oakley, "The Urban Area During Support Missions, Case Study: Mogadishu, The Strategic Level," in Russell W. Glenn (ed.), *Capital Preservation: Preparing for Urban Operations in the Twenty-First Century—Proceedings of the RAND Arroyo-TRADOC-MCWL-OSD Urban Operations Conference, March 22–23, 2000*, Santa Monica, CA: RAND Corporation, CF-162-A, 2001, p. 324.

villagers—both in the police Special Branch and psychological warfare—to other Chinese.[95]

His point is an excellent one not only from the perspective of developing an effective PSYOP campaign, but equally for collecting and processing information that could provide intelligence. That U.S. forces need to be better at "cultural intelligence" is a given. That such a capability provides an analyst to see what would be invisible to one unfamiliar with the culture in question is unquestionable. The British approach is notable in that it capitalized on the full range of language, cultural, social, and interview-based expertise. (It is also notable in that the British, as a colonial power, would in fact have had a better understanding of many languages and cultures than is typically the case with U.S. deployments. Yet Brigadier Clutterbuck still mocked even those very experienced in dealing with a foreign culture as deluding themselves.) Employing trustworthy indigenous personnel in such a manner offers tremendous dividends to the commander who develops such capabilities. For example, the Russians had considerable success in obtaining HUMINT in Chechnya when their forces contained a former Chechen mayor, Gantamirov, who was able to identify trusted agents.[96] This is certainly true for international deployments; it also has value for organizations preparing for or conducting operations involving domestic contingencies in our socially very heterogeneous cities.[97] Local police, for instance, will have a far better understanding of the immediate social and physical environment than any outsider.

---

[95] Clutterbuck, *The Long, Long War*, p. 106.

[96] Timothy L. Thomas, "Grozny 2000: Urban Combat Lessons Learned," *Military Review*, July–August 2000, pp. 50–58.

[97] There are legitimate and very significant restraints on the use of psychological operations or the collection of intelligence when operations are conducted in the United States. Issues such as whether the target of the efforts is a U.S. citizen will affect those restrictions. Generally it will not be military capabilities employed for such tasks, but homeland defense contingencies could involve the United States in support of or working with domestic agencies less bound.

It should be apparent that considerable work remains in the maturation of HUMINT doctrine. That doctrine should include not only consideration of how to best establish collection, analysis, and synthesis procedures, but also such elements as how best to assign HUMINT collection assets, where those elements should be on the battlefield, and what constitutes optimal HUMINT team organization under given conditions. Gideon Avidor suggests, for example, that HUMINT collectors should be "very close to the contact area" so that the information obtained can be disseminated in a tactically timely manner.[98]

Communications During Urban Operations

As was the case with ISR, previous RAND research in the urban operations field has investigated elements of urban communications. The results of this analysis appear in a work by Sean J. A. Edwards,[99] and are generally not repeated here. To summarize several pertinent points, the frequent line-of-sight interruptions imposed by structures, intervening walls and floors, or earth between subterranean and above-ground nodes can interfere with or entirely block vision, radio communications, GPS signals, projectile flight, or otherwise act to degrade military operations. The number of signal and emissions generators (e.g., machinery, power generation facilities, subway or bus electrical power systems, telephone or media hubs) disrupts friendly-force communications in addition to the complications it imposes on SIGINT or MASINT collection. The nature of urban structures further acts to block or cause signal strength loss in many instances (and cause propagation of reflected signals in unintended directions). Urban terrain poses these and many other impediments to consistent high-quality communications. Commanders need to determine how to overcome such problems when feasible or, as will more often be

---

[98] Gideon Avidor review notes provided to authors.

[99] Edwards, *Freeing Mercury's Wings: Improving Tactical Communications in Cities.*

the case, determine one or more alternative procedures to compensate for the loss of communications. That such problems are a factor in driving urban undertakings to more decentralized control in many cases has already been covered in considerable detail. Therefore, the consideration of communications looks briefly at those topical areas indicated in the chart.

Communications During Urban Operations

Look deeper in time and beyond military considerations during the backward planning process.	
Consider second- and higher-order effects during planning and war gaming.	
Doctrine asks lower-echelon leaders to look two levels up. Higher-echelon commanders need to consider the limits and perspectives of same nation and other subordinate headquarters and units. Commanders at every echelon need to be conscious of the situation as it impacts those at higher, lower, adjacent, joint, multinational, and interagency levels.	✔
Account for the language, cultural, procedural, and other differences that will impede the tempo and level of understanding when dealing with some coalition member units and other agencies.	✔
Be aware that urban densities compress the operational area and can result in more incidents of fratricide.	
Get the ROE right as quickly as possible.	
See the forest *and* selected trees.	

Doctrine asks lower-echelon leaders to look two levels up. Higher-echelon commanders need to consider the limits and perspectives of same nation (and other) subordinate headquarters and units.

Commanders should address these challenges in several ways. It is virtually guaranteed that a unit that has but one or two means of communicating will find itself in situations where it cannot overcome environmental conditions. Radio communications and GPS will fail. Smoke and dust will sometimes so blind soldiers that they will be unable to see even fellow squad members. Men diving for cover will likewise find themselves unable to visually acquire other unit members. The roar of combat will make verbal and other audio signals unhearable. Swirling gusts will blow smoke down streets or keep it at so low an elevation that others nearby or in the air cannot spot it. Buildings or room position will mean that flares or lasers are invisible to personnel occupying buildings. Perhaps the only compensation is that the foe suffers similarly—unless he has had the time to lay wire, is hooked into the local telephone system, or uses tactics that capitalize on nearly autonomous tactical groups. Flexibility, decentralization, and practice will be key to friendly-force success when it comes to communicating during urban contingencies. The rest of this subsection describes techniques that have proved valuable in the past.

The force should use overhead communications. Recollecting his experiences in Mogadishu, Lee Gore advised that commanders should "always have an airborne TOC. If we had an airborne TOC, [we] could talk."[100] Satellites work on a similar principle. In the future it may well be possible to employ UAVs in either a pattern or high-altitude stationary mode to provide retransmission or relay capabilities.

An alternative to airborne assets is to establish communications centers at key points of high "terrain." Retransmission or relays positioned on rooftops or other high vantage points can provide support for local communications. These positions can in turn be connected by wires or wireless connections.[101]

Personal contact may be the communications procedure of choice. Johnny Brooks, remembering his experiences in Colon, Panama, agreed fully that built-up areas pose "more line of sight problems . . . . A lot of times the battalion commander can't find his company commander, so he's going to have to go find him."[102] The disadvantage of this approach is that it can make the commander or

---

[100] Gore interview.

[101] Material from this paragraph is taken from Lt Col J. D. Wilson's comments in Jay Bruder and J. D. Wilson, interview with Gina Kingston, Quantico, Virginia, May 27, 2003.

[102] Brooks interview.

leader more vulnerable to attack or isolation from the remainder of his unit.[103]

Sean Edwards advises that cellular telephones have a number of shortfalls as a means of combat communications, including their reliance on fixed infrastructure, low data rates, and the ease of intercept and jamming.[104] However, during operations in which security issues are not a particular concern (for all or part of the undertaking, e.g., leaders might employ cell phones for communicating with PVOs or NGOs but not to discuss future plans), these and other civilian systems might be valuable augmentations to organic military capabilities. Cellular communications could be a primary means of communicating when concerns about intercept are negligible and the lack of a threat makes enemy jamming and physical destruction of base stations a nonissue.

Marines have found small, cheap squad radios of value both during peacetime trials and during combat. The off-the-shelf, short-range systems do not provide secure communications, nor are they compatible with other military systems such as those needed to call for fire support, but many find them valuable for coordinating small unit action.

Tried and true methods such as laying wire and using field telephones will still have benefits when commercial systems are down or a military-only network is desirable. This is notably the case when a unit is defending or for other reasons expecting to remain in a position for an extended period. A major advantage is the ability of hard lines to overcome line-of-sight problems. Shortfalls include chances of line breaks due to traffic or tampering, the difficulties of stringing wire across a town's or city's many streets, and the ease of tapping into the wire to monitor conversations or send false information. Wire also provides a physical connection between nodes and therefore can compromise headquarters and other important locations. The dispersion of units in urban areas means that table of organization

---

[103] John A. Simeoni, interview with Gina Kingston, Quantico, Virginia, May 27, 2003.

[104] Edwards, *Freeing Mercury's Wings: Improving Tactical Communications in Cities*, p. xiv.

and equipment quantities of wire (and, likely, the number of telephones) will fall short of needs. Quantities of wire needed to cover a given distance in a built-up area will be double to triple those needed on more open ground. The time taken to lay such lengths will obviously also be greater. Combining the military and local civilian systems can help to overcome these shortfalls. Using the telephone connection boxes located in virtually any commercial or apartment building reduces the resources that would be needed to establish a communications network in a structure's interior (though currently, there is no easy way for military wire communications systems to hook into modern systems using fiber optic cable[105]). In addition, civilian lines separated from the rest of their system can be integrated into the military network. Commercial and even barbed wire can be used in a pinch (though they will tend to require more power and are easier to tap).[106] Noninsulated wire will require those laying the system to find rubber, glass, ceramic, or similar materials to use as insulators.[107]

While the operational implications can be considerable, commanders have the option of tasking snipers to assume a retransmission role should mission requirements dictate it.

Network management is important. Units will have different communications capabilities and software, particularly during coalition operations. Unless communications are via voice, anyone sending or transmitting information is often unaware whether or not those who require the information have received it. Network management needs to provide mechanisms for determining the best ways to communicate with each unit or individual and to provide acknowledgement that communications are received.[108]

---

[105] Lester W. Grau, "Urban Warfare Communications: A Contemporary Russian View," *Red Thrust Star*, July 1996, p. 11.

[106] Ibid., pp. 6–9.

[107] Grau, "Urban Warfare Communications," pp. 6–9.

[108] Material from this paragraph is taken from Lt Col J. D. Wilson's comments in Jay Bruder and J. D. Wilson, interview with Gina Kingston, Quantico, Virginia, May 27, 2003.

Information management is no less important. Information needs to be passed to the appropriate organization or person. Detailed information should go to the commander's staff, while high-level information and information requiring a decision should often go directly to the commander. Procedures need to be developed and practiced while retaining the flexibility demanded by urban operations. When field radios were first introduced, the radio operators had to make sure that they understood a message. This meant that they needed time to develop an understanding of the context. This introduced delays of up to 45 minutes at times when, if the commanders themselves had received calls, the delay would have been minimal. Subsequent changes to procedure have largely eliminated this problem.[109]

"More is better" applies to neither information nor communications equipment during military operations. Higher headquarters need to consciously seek to aid rather than overburden subordinates. A report from the Marine Corps Systems Command Liaison Team regarding operations during the 2003 Operation Iraqi Freedom noted that "Marines were overwhelmed with the high number of varied communications equipment they were expected to use. Routinely, communicators, operations officers, and commanders found themselves in information overload as they received information over too many different networks."[110]

As is the case with many urban operations issues, the same procedures and common sense that work elsewhere need to be tailored for urban operations. The following description of a recent exercise has been sanitized, but it is offered in the spirit of precluding repeats of such procedural shortfalls:

---

[109] Jay Bruder and J. D. Wilson, interview with Gina Kingston, Quantico, Virginia, May 27, 2003.

[110] "Field Report, Central Iraq," Marine Corps Systems Command Liaison Team, April 20–25, 2003, p. 1. Online at http://www.sftt.org/PDF/article05122003a.pdf, accessed June 30, 2003.

[The brigade signal officer] said he had to put out additional re-trans[mitters], unplanned. When I asked why, he said because the buildings were causing problems with the radios that provide TOC-to-TOC connectivity. Seems the units were set up around post, generally in their own battalion areas, and had erected their [antennas] next to/behind 3 story barracks buildings. Despite a 30-foot erectable mast, the tip of the antenna was just below the rooftop. So, you guessed it, no commo. Most TOCs were less than 5 km's apart . . . . The point here is both the lack of aware-ness . . . about MOUT effects on commo [and] also our seem-ingly lacking material solutions. Also, the [communications offi-cer's] planning tools give him a range and elevation consideration when planning out his commo links, but appar-ently treats MOUT as regular terrain.[111]

Account for the language, cultural, procedural, and other differences that will impede the tempo and level of understanding when dealing with some coalition member units and other agencies.

Though digitization is becoming increasingly commonplace in the U.S. Army and the nation's other services, ours will not be a fully digitized force in the near term, if ever. Equally as important, coali-tion member armed forces will long rely on current (or even out-dated) technologies for communications, targeting, planning, and other functions. Compatibility, the specter that haunts any introduc-tion of a new system to a military inventory, is already a significant problem even within individual U.S. services. The magnitude of the disconnects increases as one considers joint, coalition, and inter-agency endeavors. A considerable number of the world's militaries rely on high frequency (HF) communications rather than the very high frequency (VHF) that characterize U.S. forces. This is especially true of African armed forces. In the event that common frequencies are found, encrypting messages sent between dissimilar systems is fre-

---

[111] Officer observations regarding an American military brigade-level command and control exercise.

quently impossible.[112] Commanders will find synchronization of actions increasingly difficult even within the U.S. military barring an effective control on acquisition or introduction of technologies that facilitate linking otherwise incompatible systems. Procedures for overcoming growing compatibility problems need to be considered before deployment and should be coordinated both within the U.S. armed services and between those services and others from coalition member nations or civilian agencies. One possibility is to better equip liaison officers, though the cost and training burdens of this option will increase dramatically as the variety of command and control systems increases. A second possibility, already discussed, is to accept some of the communications limits and establish control procedures to manage interactions.

---

[112] Harold E. Bullock, *Peace by Committee: Command and Control Issues in Multinational Peace Enforcement Operations,* thesis, Maxwell Air Force Base, AL: School of Advanced Airpower Studies, June 1994, pp. 39–40.

CHAPTER FOUR

Conclusion

Grenada, Panama, Mogadishu, and Baghdad demonstrate the increasing likelihood that urban operations will be a major if not primary component of future U.S. combat operations. Los Angeles, Port-au-Prince, and Brcko similarly demonstrate that the urban environment will be commonplace in undertakings during which combat is at most but a threat. Whether the moniker is "battle command," "mission command," "command and control," "C4ISR," or some other, the undeniable truth is evident: U.S. ground forces have to be able to provide the leadership and management requisite to success during operations in densely populated built-up areas. It is not enough to simply preclude others from suffering the life-endangering tribulations that Lieutenant Hollis and his senior leaders experienced in Somalia's capital. The sought-after state of affairs should be domination of the urban environment no less than any other. Attainment of that objective is very likely to bring with it the highly desirable result of an armed forces able to rule any battlefield much as the late-20th century American military dominated night fighting or combat in the desert.

The foregoing pages have pointed to a number of suggested actions to facilitate development of command and control capabilities that will assist in moving on this highly desirable goal. First, doctrine, both in general but more imminently and particularly for command and control, needs to make a dramatic break from its fundamentally two-party, force-on-force orientation. Conflict in the 21st century, whether involving combat or not, demonstrates more multiplicity of character than ever before. While few enemies are able to form sizable coalitions, those of which the United States is a part lack nothing for numbers. But it is perhaps in viewing the noncombatants in a theater of operations that we see the greatest demands and heterogeneity. Military operations involve numerous factions, governmental and nongovernmental representatives, and other interest groups, and it is seldom that many of these players can be or want to be represented by indigenous officials. Each one represents a potential accomplice or ally for the friendly force, complicating liaison and discrimination between those that truly share objectives with the coalition and those who seek only to promote narrower or even counterproductive agendas. Command and control doctrine, still tied to a model in which two opposing parties dominate, is inadequate to the task. It fails not only in its lack of guidance on how to handle these numerous actors, but also in its imposition of firm boundaries between actions involving combatants and those encompassing interactions with mission-relevant noncombatant representatives. Conflict embraces social, political, economic, and other realms in addition to the military, and the armed forces commander has to deal with them all. Doctrine as it currently stands fails to provide him the tutelage it should. Definitions such as that for battle command ("the exercise of command in operations *against a hostile, thinking enemy*"), center of gravity ("those characteristics, capabilities, or localities from which a *military* force, organization, or individual derives its freedom of action, physical strength, or will to fight"), and decisive points ("a geographic place, specific key event, critical system, or function that allows commanders to gain a marked advantage *over an enemy and greatly influence the outcome of an attack*") are demonstrative in this regard and require adaptation.

Inclusiveness—expanding these definitions to incorporate more than they currently do—does not mean that combat is any less demanding than it has been in the past. Nor does it imply that there is any less respect to be given the warrior and the training that prepares him. It does mean that the modern operational environment, especially the inherently heterogeneous and complex city, is more demanding of a wider range of talents. It is there that the tactical, operational, and strategic levels are most compressed, and it is therefore in the urban context that doctrine is most rigorously tested. But doctrine is only one of the several systems that require revision in light of urban demands. Those with which doctrine is so consistently and inextricably interlinked—training, technology, organization and manning, and logistics—similarly require adaptation with regard to their command and control implications. In the urban environment, too often the best course of action available to a commander is nevertheless a poor one: the least bad of the alternatives rather than inherently desirable. Training should help show the decisionmaker how to select the best of the possible choices, or at least the ones less damaging to ultimate success. This needs to begin with training commanders to think of success in terms of not only the military end state, but also the strategic end state.

Commanders need to be trained to consider the impact of their actions not only in military terms, but also in social, economic, and diplomatic terms. This includes consideration of the relationships with and between allies, the local population, local authorities, NGOs, etc. This in turn requires an understanding of second- and higher-order, or cascading, effects; that is, actions that achieve an objective in one area may have negative repercussions in others. Of particular importance is consideration of the information campaign, including the use of psychological operations and management of the media.

While the strategic end state must be considered, considerable attention must also be given to the military campaign. There may be no good location for the commander. His TOC could be too far to the rear, but moving forward will give him insight on only a small portion of his command and threatens to deny him contact with the remainder. The choice between allocating limited resources such as logistical support in a traditional manner, or weighting a main effort, or consolidating those assets in the rear is not clear cut; each has benefits as well as potentially serious negative effects. The same is true of a reserve. The penalties are no different than in other environments, but the delays in moving it forward to the critical point on the battlefield when needed or having it bypassed if too far forward loom greater in a city. Training needs to help with these and other difficult decisions, such as how to monitor and control a truly three-dimensional battlefield. True, mountains have three dimensions, but a commander can by and large monitor them on a two-dimensional map. The same is true of a jungle, but far less so in a city with high-rise buildings in the area of operations. Training needs to similarly prepare the leaders and the led to deal with the extended travel times, intermittent communications, and perishable nature of situational awareness intelligence inherent in the high-density environment characteristic of built-up areas. Decentralized operations may become the norm; leaders and those that might replace them given high urban casualty rates need to be trained for such approaches. Units with leaders and soldiers untrained for such demands are organizations unprepared for urban combat.

Similar consideration should be given to the application of currently available technologies and those yet to be acquired. The problems of intermittent lines-of-sight and broken communications links can sometimes be overcome through the use of directional antennas or knowing how to "bounce" radio signals off buildings. It is also important to recognize the limitations inherent in current systems and prepare command and control procedures to mitigate their negative effects. These immediate adjustments have longer-term complements. Acquisition of systems without regard to urban implications is unforgivable given the evolving nature of the modern battlefield. Current acoustic and vibratory sensors are too often fooled by reflections off buildings or other hard surfaces. Standards to compensate for this shortcoming should be included in development guidance now. Though an imperfect solution, overhead signal relays and/or retransmission capabilities such as UAVs, lighter-than air systems, or satellites could assist in overcoming line-of-sight limitations affecting radios and GPS. Artificial line-of-sight mechanisms as simple as relays placed at corners when soldiers move through a building, thereby allowing radio signals to "turn a corner," would also have benefit. Inertial systems that combine enhanced capabilities to compensate for an infantryman's tumbling through doorways and rolling right or left with an as-available GPS update would help defeat the inability to monitor friendly-force locations when soldiers or marines enter subterranean passageways or buildings. It is a given that the greater density of friendly forces in an urban environment is likely to cause overlapping radio frequencies and interference, especially within coalition member units less well equipped than U.S. forces. [1] The time to address these inevitabilities is now rather than when they occur during active operations. Means of better queuing HUMINT to other collection systems and vice versa are likewise an outstanding requirement if ISR needs are to be met.

Training and the development of appropriate organizational and manning capabilities are linked. The lieutenants of tomorrow should not suffer the same unfamiliarity with coalition member equipment as did Lieutenant Hollis in Mogadishu. American soldiers should not be seeing fellow U.S. warriors in dismounted or mechanized units for the first time as did those of Lieutenant Colonel Clark in Somalia after October 3–4, 1993. Training, doctrine, and (if necessary) modifications to current organizational structures are necessary so that commanders will know how to allocate their often too scarce logistics and other assets. The evolution of manning and equipment capabilities that allow a rapid, effective, and timely transition from combat to stability or support-dominated operations is long overdue. Recent challenges in Baghdad in this regard demonstrate the necessity to develop doctrine for and war game when the logistics pipeline should begin to change its "settings" so as to provide a mixture leaner in combat assets and richer in those better suited for urban infrastructure and other nation-building tasks. These are difficult command decisions, and they are rarely practiced other than during actual operations. Recent American and Australian contingencies demonstrate a need for better liaison with other coalition units, PVO and NGO representatives, and local governmental and nongovernmental organizations, yet liaison efforts continue more often than not to be under-

---

[1] Procedures have been developed to address these challenges under the moniker of "spectrum management." Responsibility for this development and the evolution of the procedures belongs to the C16 staff section in the role of central manager.

manned, underequipped, and ad hoc in character. The time to consider such problems is now. Commanders will have sufficient challenges on hand during operations without having to find last-minute solutions to such organizational and logistical issues.

These many difficulties are not insurmountable. The foregoing pages include seven primary recommendations to address these and the many other mission implications confronted in attempting to command and control urban contingencies:

1. Look deeper in time and beyond military considerations during the backward planning process.

2. Consider second- and higher-order effects during planning and war gaming.

3. Doctrine asks lower-echelon leaders to look two levels up. Higher-echelon commanders need to consider the limits and perspectives of same nation (and other) subordinate headquarters and units. Commanders at every echelon need to be conscious of the situation as it impacts those at higher, lower, adjacent, joint, multinational, and interagency levels.

4. Account for the language, cultural, procedural, and other differences that will impede the tempo and level of understanding when dealing with some coalition member units and other agencies.

5. Be aware that urban densities compress the operational area and can result in more incidents of fratricide.

6. Get the ROE right as quickly as possible.

7. See the forest *and* selected trees.

These recommendations are derivative of history's lessons, common sense, and years of considering the demands of command and control during urban contingencies. Together they are like a good plan for battle. While the details may not survive the first minutes of an operation, they provide a far better beginning point for adaptation than a blank slate.

Bibliography

Books

Adkin, Mark, *Urgent Fury: The Battle for Grenada*, London: Leo Cooper, 1989.

Alberts, David S., John J. Garstka, and Frederick P. Stein, *Network Centric Warfare: Developing and Levering Information Superiority*, 2nd ed., Washington, D.C.: CCRP Publication Series, 2002.

Alberts, David S., and Richard E. Hayes, *Power to the Edge: Command and Control in the Information Age*, Washington, D.C.: CCRP Publication Series, 2003.

Breen, Bob, *A Little Bit of Hope: Australian Force—Somalia*, St. Leonards, Australia: Allen & Unwin, 1998.

Breen, Bob, *Mission Accomplished, East Timor: The Australian Defence Force Participation in the International Forces East Timor (INTERFET)*, Crows Nest, Australia: Allen & Unwin, 2000.

Chuikov, Vasili I., *The Battle for Stalingrad*, New York: Holt, Rinehart, and Winston, 1964.

Von Clausewitz, Carl, *On War*, Princeton: Princeton University Press, 1976.

Clutterbuck, Richard L., *The Long, Long War: Counterinsurgency in Malaya and Vietnam*, New York: Praeger, 1966.

Desch, Michael C. (ed), *Soldiers in Cities: Military Operations on Urban Terrain*, Carlisle Barracks, PA: Strategic Studies Institute, U.S. Army War College, 2001.

Huntington, Samuel P., *The Soldier and the State: The Theory and Politics of Civil-Military Relations*, New York: Vintage, 1957.

Khuri, Fuad I., *From Village to Suburb: Order and Change in Greater Beirut*, Chicago: University of Chicago Press, 1975.

Smith, Edward A., Jr., *Effects Based Operations: Applying Network Centric Warfare in Peace, Crisis and War*, Washington, D.C.: CCRP Publication Series, 2002.

Articles

Burger, Kim, "US Army Future Combat Systems," *Jane's Defence Weekly*, Vol. 35, June 13, 2001, pp. 20–27.

Caterinicchia, Dan, "Army considers urban warfare tech," *Federal Computer Week*, January 6, 2003. Online at http://www.fcw.com/fcw/articles/2003/0106/web-cecom-01-06-03.asp, accessed June 25, 2003.

Dwyer, Jim, Kevin Flynn, and Ford Fessenden, "9/11 Exposed Deadly Flaws in Rescue Plan," *The New York Times*, July 7, 2002. Online at http://www.nytimes.com/2002/07/07/nyreg.../07emer.html, accessed April 22, 2003.

"Experiment Results Show Room For Improvement in the Digital Army," *Inside the Army*, July 23, 2001, p. 5.

Grau, Lester W., "Urban Warfare Communications: A Contemporary Russian View," *Red Thrust Star*, July 1996, pp. 4–12.

Hoar, Joseph P., "A CINC's Perspective," *Joint Forces Quarterly*, Autumn 1993, pp. 56–63.

Hollis, Mark A. B., "Platoon Under Fire: Mogadishu, October 1993," *Infantry*, January–April 1998, pp. 27–34.

Honore, Russel L., "Battle Command," *Military Review*, Vol. 82, September–October 2002, pp. 10–15.

Kendrick, William A., "Peacekeeping Operations in Somalia," *Infantry*, May–June 1995, pp. 31–35.

Krulak, Charles C., "The Strategic Corporal: Leadership in the Three Block War," *Marines Magazine*, January 1999, pp. 28–34.

LeGare, Marc, "Battle Command and Visualization," *Military Review*, Vol. 82, September–October 2002, pp. 16–21.

Melvin, R. A. M. S., "Mission Command," *British Army Review*, Autumn 2002, pp. 4–9.

"More Bombs on Target: Laser targeting pod improves B-52 precision-strike capability," *Citizen Airman*, June 2003.

"Soft radios," *The Economist Technology Quarterly*, in *The Economist*, Vol. 357, December 9, 2000, p. 7.

Solomon, Billy K., "Improving Maneuver Sustainment for the Objective Force," *Army Logistician*, Vol. 34, November–December 2002, pp. 2–7.

Spencer, David E., "Urban Combat Doctrine of the Salvadoran FMLN," *Infantry*, November–December 1990, pp. 17–19.

Stanton, Martin N., "Riot Control for the 1990s," *Infantry*, January–February 1996, pp. 22–29.

Strader, O. Kent, "Counterinsurgency in an Urban Environment," *Infantry*, January–February 1997, pp. 8–11.

Thomas, Timothy L., "Grozny 2000: Urban Combat Lessons Learned," *Military Review*, July–August 2000, pp. 50–58.

Wall, Robert, "Litening Strikes: As combat operations in Iraq wind down, B-52/Litening combo makes debut," *Aviation Week & Space Technology*, April 28, 2003, p. 35.

Wenger, William V., "The Los Angeles Riots: A Battalion Commander's Perspective," *Infantry*, January–February 1994, pp. 13–16.

Zolli, Andrew, "Oh, Nooo! What If GPS Fails?" *Wired*, Vol. 11, May 2003, p. 40.

Reports, Manuals, and Miscellaneous

Allard, Kenneth, *Somalia Operations: Lessons Learned*, Fort McNair, Washington, D.C.: National Defense University Press, 1995.

"Ambush in Mogadishu: Interview—General Thomas Montgomery (Ret.)," *Frontline*, Public Broadcasting System, undated. Online at http://www.pbs.org/wgbh/pages/frontline/shows/ambush/interviews/montgomery.html, accessed May 30, 2003.

Army Field Manual Volume 2, Operations in Specific Environments, Part 5, *Urban Operations*, British Army, 1999.

Battle Command Techniques and Procedures: A Commander's Guide for the Coordination and Execution of Battlefield Operating Systems, First Coordinating Draft, Fort Monroe, VA: U.S. Army Training and Doctrine Command, April 21, 1995.

Battle Command: Leadership and Decision Making for War and Operations Other Than War (Draft 2.1), Fort Leavenworth, KS: Battle Command Battle Laboratory, April 22, 1994.

Board of Inquiry—Croatia: CF Operations in the Balkans 1991–1995, last modified November 12, 2002. Online at www.dnd.ca/hr/boi/engraph/about_boi_e.asp, accessed April 22, 2003.

Bullock, Harold E., *Peace by Committee: Command and Control Issues in Multinational Peace Enforcement Operations,* thesis, Maxwell Air Force Base, AL: School of Advanced Airpower Studies, June 1994.

C4ISR Handbook for Integrated Planning (CHIP), Washington, D.C.: Office of the Assistant Secretary of Defense, April 17, 1998.

Cebrowski, Arthur K., and John J. Garstka, "Network-Centric Warfare: Its Origin and Future," *Naval Institute Proceedings.* Online at www.usni.org/Proceedings/Articles98/PROcebrowski.htm, accessed April 10, 2003.

Chura, Michael F., "Mission Command and UO," email to Russell W. Glenn, March 15, 2003.

Chura, Michael F., "Some Thoughts on Urban Battle Command in the Twenty-First Century," email to Dr. Russell W. Glenn, December 15, 2003.

Conner, Bill, "battle command," email to Russell W. Glenn, December 11, 2002.

Cooling, Norman L., *Shaping the Battlespace to Win the Street Fight,* thesis, Fort Leavenworth, KS: School of Advanced Military Studies, 2000.

Cordesman, Anthony H., *The "Instant Lessons" of the Iraq War: Main Report* (Third Working Draft), Washington, D.C.: Center for Strategic and International Studies, April 14, 2003.

Day, Clifford E., *Critical Analysis on the Defeat of Task Force Ranger,* research paper, Montgomery Air Force Base, AL: Air Command and Staff College, March 1997.

Darilek, Richard, Walt L. Perry, Jerome Bracken, John Gordon, and Brian Nichiporuk, *Measures of Effectiveness for the Information-Age Army*, Santa Monica, CA: RAND Corporation, MR-1155-A, 2001.

Don, Bruce W., John A. Friel, Thomas J. Herbert, and Jerry M. Sollinger, *Future Ground Commanders' Close Support Needs and Desirable System Characteristics*, Santa Monica, CA: RAND Corporation, MR-833-OSD, 2002.

Edwards, Sean J. A., *Freeing Mercury's Wings: Improving Tactical Communications in Cities*, Santa Monica, CA: RAND Corporation, MR-1316-A, 2001.

Eicke, John, "Army G2 ISR Workshop & Sensors for Urban Operations," briefing presented at Urban ISR Briefing, George Washington University, Washington, D.C., March 21, 2003.

Field Manual 1-111, *Aviation Brigades*, Washington, D.C.: Headquarters, Department of the Army, October 27, 1997. Online at http://www.adtdl.army.mil/cgi-bin/atdl.dll/fm/1-111, accessed May 7, 2003.

Field Manual 3-0, *Operations*, Washington, D.C.: Headquarters, Department of the Army, June 2001.

Field Manual 3-06, *Urban Operations*, Washington, D.C.: Headquarters, Department of the Army, June 2003.

Field Manual 3-06.1, *Aviation Urban Operations: Multiservice Procedures for Aviation Urban Operations*, Fort Monroe, VA: U.S. Army Training and Doctrine Command, April 2001.

Field Manual 3-06.11, *Combined Arms Operations in Urban Terrain*, Washington, D.C.: Headquarters, Department of the Army, February 28, 2002.

Field Manual 3-20.96, *RSTA Squadron*, 2nd Coordinating Draft, Fort Knox, KY: U.S. Army Armor Center, undated.

Field Manual 6-0, *Mission Command: Command and Control of Army Forces* [approved final draft], Washington, D.C.: Headquarters, Department of the Army, October 2002.

"Field Report, Central Iraq," Marine Corps Systems Command Liaison Team, April 20–25, 2003. Online at http://www.sftt.org/PDF/article05122003a.pdf, accessed June 30, 2003.

Francey, Richard M., "Precision Fire Support for MOUT," monograph, Fort Leavenworth, KS: School of Advanced Military Studies, November 29, 1994.

Gellert, Frederick, "MOUT Experience (or lack thereof)," email to Russell W. Glenn, April 14, 2002.

Gellert, Frederick, "MOUT Experience (or lack thereof)," email to Russell W. Glenn, April 15, 2002.

"General Anthony Zinni's MOOTW Considerations Make Sense." Online at http://www.urbanoperations.dom/zinni.htm, accessed May 26, 2003.

Glenn, Russell W., *Managing Complexity During Urban Operations: Visualizing the Elephant*, Santa Monica, CA: RAND Corporation, DB-430-A, 2004.

Glenn, Russell W., ed., *Capital Preservation: Preparing for Urban Operations in the Twenty-First Century: Proceedings of the RAND Arroyo-TRADOC-MCWL-OSD Urban Operations Conference, March 22–23, 2000*, Santa Monica, CA: RAND Corporation, CF-162-A, 2001.

Glenn, Russell W., (ed.), *Ready for Armageddon: Proceedings of the 2001 RAND Arroyo-U.S. Army ACTD-CETO-USMC Non-Lethal and Urban Operations Program Urban Operations Conference*, Santa Monica, CA: RAND Corporation, CF-179-A, 2002.

Glenn, Russell W., Sean J. A. Edwards, David Johnson, Jay Bruder, Michael L. Scheiern, Elwyn D. Harris, Jody A. Jacobs, Iris Kameny, and John Pinder, *Getting the Musicians of Mars on the Same Sheet of Music: Army Joint, Multinational, and Interagency C4ISR Interoperability*, Santa Monica, CA: RAND Corporation, DB-288-A, 2000, For Official Use Only.

Glenn, Russell W., Steven L. Hartman, and Scott Gerwehr, *Urban Combat Service Support Operations: The Shoulders of Atlas*, Santa Monica, CA: RAND Corporation, MR-1717-A, 2004.

Glenn, Russell W., Jamison Jo Medby, Scott Gerwehr, Frederick J. Gellert, and Andrew O'Donnell, *Honing the Keys to the City: Refining the United States Marine Corps Reconnaissance Force for Urban Ground Operations*, Santa Monica, CA: RAND Corporation, MR-1628-USMC, 2003.

Goodson, Carl, and Cynthia Brakhage, *Fireground Support Operations*, 1st ed., International Fire Service Training Association, Fire Protection Publications, Oklahoma State University, March 2002.

Hammond, Ralph, "Operation Iraqi Freedom, Task Force 2-7 Infantry (Mechanized) After Action Review," Fort Benning, GA: Combined Arms and Tactics Directorate, U.S. Infantry School, undated.

Harris, Aidan, *Improving the Infantry's Inventory: Can New Technologies Transform Military Operations in Urban Terrain?*, Lancaster, UK: Lancaster University, March 2003.

Hawley, Chris, Gregory G. Noll, and Michael S. Hildebrand, *Special Operations, for Terrorism and Hazmat Crimes,* 1st ed., Red Hat Publishing Company, Inc., Library of Congress number 2001 132074, 2002.

Hicks, J. Marcus, *Fire in the City: Airpower in Urban, Smaller-Scale Contingencies*, thesis, Fort Leavenworth, KS: School of Advanced Military Studies, June 1999.

"Iraq's New Chiefs Emerge from Shadow—In Mosul, U.S. Alliance with Militia Leader Shows How Power Is Brokered," *The Wall Street Journal*, May 27, 2003.

JAC(02)11, *Industrial Action by the Fire Brigades Union, Contingency Arrangements During the 8-Day Strike, 22–30 November 2002, COBR—Joint Assessment Cell Report,* UK Cabinet Office, December 2, 2002.

Jakubowski, Greg, and Mike Morton, *Rapid Intervention Teams,* Fire Protection Publications, Oklahoma State University, Library of Congress Control Number 2001 130285, 2002.

Joint Publication 1-02, *Department of Defense Dictionary of Military and Associated Terms,* Washington, D.C.: Joint Chiefs of Staff, April 12, 2001 (as amended through May 23, 2003).

Joint Publication 3-06, *Doctrine for Joint Urban Operations*, Washington, D.C.: Joint Chiefs of Staff, September 16, 2002.

Létourneau, François, "Different Approaches for the Creation and Exploitation of 3D Urban Models," *International Command Control Research and Technology Symposium*, Quebec City: Command and Control Research Program, September 2002.

Logistics in a Peace Enforcement Environment: Operation Continue Hope Lessons Learned, Fort Leavenworth, KS: U.S. Army Center for Army Lessons Learned, November 16, 1993.

Marine Corps Warfighting Publication 3-35.3, *Military Operations on Urbanized Terrain (MOUT)*, Washington, D.C.: Headquarters, United States Marine Corps, April 15, 1998.

Marlowe, David H., *Psychological and Psychosocial Consequences of Combat and Deployment with Special Emphasis on the Gulf War*, Santa Monica, CA: RAND Corporation, MR-1018/11-OSD, 2001.

Matsumura, John, Randall Steeb, Thomas J. Herbert, John Gordon, Carl A. Rhodes, Russell W. Glenn, Mike Barbero, Fred Gellert, Phyllis Kantar, Gail Halverson, Robert Cochran, and Paul Steinberg, *Exploring Advanced Technologies for the Future Combat Systems Program*, Santa Monica, CA: RAND Corporation, MR-1332-A, 2002.

Matsumura, John, Randall Steeb, Randall G. Bowdish, Scot Eisenhard, Gail Halverson, Thomas J. Herbert, Mark R. Lees, and John Pinder, *Rapid Force Projection Technologies: Assessing the Performance of Advanced Ground Sensors*, Santa Monica, CA: RAND Corporation, DB-262-A/OSD, 2000.

McCann, Carol M., "Command: the Core of C2," *International Command Control Research and Technology Symposium*, Quebec City: Command and Control Research Program, September 2002.

Medby, Jamie, "a few answers for you," email to Russell W. Glenn, May 23, 2000.

National Fire Service, Incident Management System, *Model Procedures Guide for High-Rise Fire Fighting*, 1st ed., National Fire Service Incident Management System Consortium Model Procedures Committee, Library of Congress Number 96-61972.

National Fire Service Incident Management System, *Model Procedures Guide for Structural Firefighting*, 2nd ed., Fire Protection Publications, Oklahoma State University, Library of Congress Number 00-107086.

National Fire Service Incident Management System, *Structural Collapse and US&R Operations*, 1st ed., National Fire Service Incident Management Systems Consortium Model Procedures Committee, Fire Protection Publications, Oklahoma State University, Library of Congress Number 98-86963.

Neiman, Max, "Urban Operations: Social Meaning, the Urban Built Forms and Economic Function," Chapter 10, in Desch, Michael C., ed., *Soldiers in Cities: Military Operations on Urban Terrain*, Carlisle Barracks, PA: Strategic Studies Institute, U. S. Army War College, 2001.

Objective Force Task Force, *The Objective Force in 2015*, white paper, final draft, December 8, 2002.

Operational Guidelines for Urban Communications, Quantico, VA: Naval Ocean Systems Command, October 14, 1983.

"Operation Continue Hope II: Mechanized Perspective," briefing, no organization specified, undated. Online at http://www.infantry.army.mil/catd/urban_ops/, accessed April 20, 2003.

Phelps, Burton, and Robert Murgallis, *Command and Control, ICS, Strategy Development and Tactical Selections,* 1st ed., Fire Protection Publications, Oklahoma State University, Library of Congress Control Number 2001 1097419, January 2002.

Pigeon, Luc, Clark J. Beamish, and Michel Zybala, *HUMINT Communication Information Systems for Complex Warfare*, Quebec: Defence R&D Canada Valcartier, undated.

Posen, Barry, "Urban Operations: Tactical Realities and Strategic Ambiguities," Chapter 11 in Desch, Michael C., ed., *Soldiers in Cities: Military Operations on Urban Terrain*, Carlisle Barracks, PA: Strategic Studies Institute, U.S. Army War College, 2001.

Potts, David, ed., *The Big Issue: Command and Combat in the Information Age*, The Strategic and Combat Studies Institute Occasional Paper Number 45, March 2002.

"Press Conference by the President," Office of the Press Secretary, The White House, 10:21 AM EDT, October 14, 1993. Online at http://clinton6.nara.gov/1993/10/1993-10-14-presidents-press-conference.html, accessed May 30, 2003.

Rafferty, Russell, "OIF Marine Recap," email to Russell W. Glenn, June 6, 2003.

Reardon, Mark, "IO and 'Urban Warrior,'" email to Russell W. Glenn, March 26, 1999.

Rutter, Scott E., et al., *Operation Iraqi Freedom: Task Force 2-7 Infantry (Mechanized)*, undated.

Ryan, Alan, "Primary Responsibilities and Primary Risks," *Australian Defence Force Participation in the International Force East Timor*, Land Warfare Studies Centre Study Paper No. 304, November 2000.

Sampson, M. T., and J. R. Parrington, *Qualitative Assessment Report: The Close Air Support (CAS) Survey*, Yuma, AZ: Marine Aviation Weapons and Tactics Squadron One, February 1, 1999.

Sundin, Claes, and Henrik Friman, eds., *ROLF 2010: the Way Ahead and the First Step—A Collection of Research Papers*, Stockholm: The Swedish National Defence College, 2000.

TRADOC Pamphlet 525-4-0, *The United States Army Objective Force Maneuver Sustainment Support Concept*, Fort Monroe, VA: U.S. Army Training and Doctrine Command, Version 12-03-01a.

"Urban Operation Lessons Learned TTPs," briefing, no organization specified, undated. Online at http://www.infantry.army.mil/catd/urban_ops/, accessed April 20, 2003.

"Urban Patrolling I: Student Handout," Quantico, VA: United States Marine Corps Basic Officer Course, undated. Online at http://www.mcu.usmc.mil/tbsnew/boc.htm, could no longer be accessed as of April 22, 2003.

Interviews

Allison, John, with Gina Kingston, Arlington, VA, June 6, 2003.

Allison, John, with Todd Helmus, Arlington VA, June 5, 2003.

Brooks, Johnny, with Russell W. Glenn, Fort Benning, GA, April 4, 2003.

Bruder, Jay, and J. D. Wilson, with Gina Kingston, Quantico, VA, May 27, 2003.

Gore, Lee, with Russell W. Glenn, Atlanta, GA, April 2, 2003.

Miller, John P., with Russell W Glenn, Gina Kingston, Les Dishman, and Steve Hartman, Hollywood, CA, May 15, 2003.

Ridenour, Doug, and Jared L. Ware, with Gina Kingston, Arlington, VA., June 4, 2003.

Simeoni, John A., with Gina Kingston, Quantico, VA, May 27, 2003.

Zaken, Nachum, with Russell W. Glenn, Latrun, Israel, April 10, 2000.